Favorite
Christian
Poems

Favorite
Christian
Poems

~~~~~~

Compiled and Edited by

Donald T. Kauffman

Fleming H. Revell Company
Old Tappan, New Jersey

Acknowledgments

Acknowledgment is made for use of material by the following authors:

Amy Carmichael, TOWARD JERUSALEM. Selections used by permission of the publisher, The Society for Promoting Christian Knowledge.

Sybil L. Armes for poems from DEVOTIONS FROM A GRATEFUL HEART and DEVOTIONS FOR DYNAMIC LIVING, published by Fleming H. Revell Co., one from SUNRISE TO STARLIGHT published by Abingdon Press, and one from *The Radiant Trail* (Nashville: Broadman Press, 1947), p. 4. Used by permission.

Annie Johnson Flint, Copyright Evangelical Publishers, Toronto, Canada. Reproduced by permission.

Ralph S. Cushman, "The Secret" from SPIRITUAL HILLTOPS, published by Abingdon Press.

Minnie L. Haskins, "The Gate of the Year." Used by permission of Christy and Moore, Ltd.

Lona Fowler, "Middle-Time."

Myra Brooks Welch, "The Touch of the Master's Hand," © 1943 by the Brethren Press. Used by permission.

A. B. Simpson, "Get Somewhere" from SONGS OF THE SPIRIT. Used by permission of Christian Publications, Inc., Harrisburg, Pennsylvania.

Frances McKinnon Morton, "The Meaning of Prayer" from the SECRET PLACE, American Baptist Board of Education and Publication, Valley Forge, Pennsylvania. Used by permission.

Martha Snell Nicholson, "Loveliness," "Dominion," "Bible Study," "Two Homes," "On a Sick Bed," "Dying," "Altars Raised to God," and "Prayer for a New House," © 1938, found in *Wings and Sky*. By permission of Moody Press.

Frances Stoakley Lankford, "Prayer at a Nursery Window." Used by permission of "Spirit," a magazine of poetry.

Mary S. Edgar, "God Who Touchest Earth with Beauty."

Diligent effort has been made to locate and secure permission for the inclusion of all copyrighted material in this book. If any such acknowledgments have been omitted, the compiler and publishers would appreciate receiving full information so that proper credit may be given in future editions.

To my father
who loved good books

Foreword

One of the old books I value more than many of the new ones in my library comes from my father's Pennsylvania Dutch childhood. An inscription on the flyleaf reads:

"Presented to D. C. Kauffman by his Sunday School teacher, Miss Hallie Sourbeer, for reading the Bible every day for one year. May 27, 1889."

The book is an anthology of Christian poems.

My own childhood was deeply influenced by the Bible and Christian poems and hymns. Throughout my life I have been impressed by the inadequacy of mere prose to communicate the glories of Christian truth—by the tendency of Christian writers, from St. Paul to Fanny Crosby, Annie Johnson Flint, and C. S. Lewis, to give their words wings. I have tried to assemble here some of the best loved and most enduring of these poems. It would be impossible to name all those who have contributed in one way or another to this anthology, but I wish to mention particularly my father, my mother, my father-in-law, my mother-in-law, my wife (a special admirer of Amy Carmichael, Lona Fowler, and George Macdonald) and my daughter Cynthia. Cynthia's painstaking assistance aided greatly in the preparation of the manuscript.

May the poems in this book become new favorites of those not yet familiar with them, and continue to give many readers light and joy.

Donald T. Kauffman

Contents

CONTENTS

Favorite
Christian
Poems

ADORATION

For the Lord is great, and greatly to be praised
—Psalm 96:4

LOVELINESS

When God invented beauty,
He made such lovely things!
My happy heart is soaring
With every bird that wings.

The sea is His, He made it,
His handiwork the moon
And all the stars of heaven,
The sun that shines at noon.

His master brush spreads colors
On palettes of the skies,
And over ripening grain fields
The haze of autumn lies.

He gave us for our pleasure
Each lovely flower that blows,
Then added for good measure
The perfume of the rose.

He knows the singing rapture
That comes with each new Spring . . .
O, when God gave us beauty
He made a wondrous thing!
—Martha Snell Nicholson

HOLY, HOLY, HOLY

Holy, holy, holy! Lord God Almighty!
All thy works shall praise Thy name,
In earth, and sky, and sea;

Holy, holy, holy, merciful and mighty!
God in Three Persons,
Blessed Trinity!
—*Reginald Heber*

GOD OF THE NEBULÆ

Lover of all, I hold me fast by Thee,
Ruler of time, King of eternity
There is no great with Thee, there is no small,
For Thou art all, and fillest all in all.

The new-born world swings forth at Thy command,
The falling dewdrop falls into Thy hand.
God of the firmament's mysterious powers,
I see Thee thread the minutes of my hours.

I see Thee guide the frail, the fading moon
That walks alone through empty skies at noon.
Was ever way-worn, lonely traveller
But had Thee by him, blessèd Comforter?

Out of my vision swims the untracked star,
Thy counsels too are high and very far,
Only I know, God of the nebulæ,
It is enough to hold me fast by Thee.
—*Amy Carmichael*

HE GIVETH MORE

He giveth more grace when the burdens grow greater,
    He sendeth more strength when the labors increase;
To added affliction He addeth His mercy,
    To multiplied trials, His multiplied peace.

When we have exhausted our store of endurance,
    When our strength has failed ere the day is half done,

When we reach the end of our hoarded resources,
   Our Father's full giving is only begun.

His love has no limit, His grace has no measure,
   His power no boundary known unto men;
For out of His infinite riches in Jesus
   He giveth and giveth and giveth again.
                              —*Annie Johnson Flint*

"THE HEAVENS DECLARE THE GLORY OF GOD"

   You ask me how I know it's true
      That there is a living God—
   A God who rules the universe,
      The sky . . . the sea . . . the sod;
   A God who holds all creatures
      In the hollow of His hand;
   A God who put *Infinity*
      In one tiny grain of sand;
   A God who made the seasons—
      Winter, Summer, Fall and Spring,
   And put His flawless rhythm
      Into each created thing;
   A God who hangs the sun out
      Slowly with the break of day,
   And gently takes the stars in
      And puts the night away;
   A God whose mighty handiwork
      Defies the skill of man,
   For no architect can alter
      God's *Perfect Master Plan*—
   What better answers are there
      To prove His Holy Being
   Than the wonders all around us
      That are ours just for the seeing.
                              —*Helen Steiner Rice*

THE HOLY OF HOLIES

"Elder Father, though thine eyes
Shine with hoary mysteries,
Canst thou tell what in the heart
Of a cowslip blossom lies?"

"Smaller than all lives that be
Secret as the deepest sea,
Stands a little house of seeds
Like an elfin's granary."

"Speller of the stones and weeds
Skilled in Nature's crafts and creeds,
Tell me what is in the heart
Of the smallest of the seeds."

"God Almighty, and with Him
Cherubim and Seraphim,
Filling all eternity,
Adonai Elohim!"

—*G. K. Chesterton*

PRAISE THE LORD

Let us with a gladsome mind
Praise the Lord for He is kind;
For His mercies aye endure,
Ever faithful, ever sure.

Let us blaze His name abroad,
For of gods He is the God;
Who by all-commanding might,
Filled the new-made world with light.

He the golden tressed sun
Caused all day his course to run;
Th' horned moon to shine by night,
'Mid her spangled sisters bright.

He His chosen race did bless,
In the wasteful wilderness;
He hath, with a piteous eye,
Looked upon our misery.

All things living He doth feed.
His full hand supplies their need;
For His mercies aye endure,
Ever faithful, ever sure.

—*John Milton*

GOD'S GRANDEUR

The world is charged with the grandeur of God.
It will flame out, like shining from shook foil;
It gathers to a greatness, like the ooze of oil
Crushed. Why do men then now not reck his rod?
Generations have trod, have trod, have trod;
And all is seared with trade; bleared, smeared with toil;
And wears man's smudge and shares man's smell: the soil
Is bare now, nor can foot feel, being shod.

And for all this, nature is never spent;
There lives the dearest freshness deep down things;
And through the last lights off the black West went
Oh, morning, at the brown brink eastward, springs—
Because the Holy Ghost over the bent
World broods with warm breast and with ah! bright wings.

—*Gerard Manley Hopkins*

"MY SOUL DOTH MAGNIFY THE LORD"

My soul shall be a telescope,
    Searching the distant bounds of time and space,
That somehow I may image, as I grope,
    Jehovah's power and grace.

My soul a microscope shall be,
  In all minutest providences keen
Jehovah's patient thoughtfulness to see,
  And read His love between.

My soul shall be a burning-glass,
  That diligence to worship may succeed,
That I may catch God's glories as they pass,
  And focus to a deed.

So, even so,
  A mote in His creation, even I,
Seeking alone to do, to feel, to know,
  The Lord must magnify.

—*Amos R. Wells*

How Can I Keep From Singing?

My life flows on in endless song; above earth's lamentation
  I catch the sweet, though far-off hymn that hails a new creation.
Thro' all the tumult and the strife I hear the music ringing;
  It finds an echo in my soul—how can I keep from singing?

What though my joys and comforts die? The Lord my Saviour liveth!
  What though the darkness gather 'round? Songs in the night he
    giveth!
No storm can shake my inmost calm, while to that refuge clinging;
  Since Christ is Lord of heaven and earth, how can I keep from
    singing?

I lift my eyes; the cloud grows thin, I see the blue above it;
  And day by day this pathway smooths, since first I learned to
    love it.
The peace of Christ makes fresh my heart, a fountain ever springing;
  All things are mine since I am his—how can I keep from singing?

Praise to Thee

I offer Thee—
Every flower that ever grew,

Every bird that ever flew,
Every wind that ever blew:
　　　Good God!
Every thunder rolling,
Every church bell tolling,
Every leaf and sod:
　　　　I praise Thee!
I offer Thee—
Every wave that ever moved,
Every heart that ever loved,
Thee, thy Father's Well-Beloved,
　　　　Dear Lord.
Every river dashing,
Every lightning flashing,
Like an angel's sword:
　　　　I bless Thee.
I offer Thee—
Every cloud that ever swept
O'er the skies, and broke and wept
In rain, and with the flowerets slept:
　　　　My King!
Each communicant praying,
Every angel staying
Before thy throne to sing:
　　　　I adore Thee!
I offer Thee—
Every flake of virgin snow,
Every spring of earth below,
Every human joy and woe,
　　　　My Love!
O Lord! And all Thy glorious
Self o'er death victorious,
Throned in heaven above:
　　　　I glorify Thee!
　　　　　—Ancient Irish Prayer

AGE

But the path of the just is as the shining light that shineth more and more unto the perfect day
                                                    —Proverbs 4:18

SAVED BY GRACE

Some day the silver cord will break,
And I no more as now shall sing;
But O, the joy when I shall wake
Within the palace of the King!

And I shall see Him face to face,
And tell the story—Saved by grace;
And I shall see Him face to face,
And tell the story—Saved by grace.

Some day my earthly house will fall,
I cannot tell how soon 'twill be,
But this I know—my All in All
Has now a place in heaven for me.

Some day, when fades the golden sun
Beneath the rosy-tinted west,
My blessed Lord will say, "Well done!"
And I shall enter into rest.

Some day: till then I'll watch and wait,
My lamp all trimmed and burning bright,
That when my Saviour opes the gate,
My soul to Him may take its flight.
                                    —Fanny J. Crosby

AUTUMN

Great Giver of my lovely green in Spring,
    A dancing, singing green upon my tree,
My green has passed; I have no song to sing,
    What will my Autumn be?

Must it be, though alive, as all but dead,
   A heavy-footed and a silent thing?
Effectless, sapless, tedious, limited,
   A withered vanishing?

Thus I; but He to me: Have I not shown
   In Autumn woodland and on mountain fell,
The splendour of My purpose for Mine own?
   Fear not, for all is well.

And thou shalt see, My child, what I will do,
   For as thy lingering Autumn days unfold,
The lovely, singing green of hitherto
   Will come to thee in gold.
                —Amy Carmichael

AS I GROW OLD

God keep my heart attuned to laughter
   When youth is done;
When all the days are gray days, coming after
   The warmth, the sun.
God keep me then from bitterness, from grieving,
   When life seems cold;
God keep me always loving and believing
   As I grow old.

FALLING LEAVES

I saw you fall but a moment ago,
   Dear leaf of crimson hue;
The summer is past, and the bosom of earth
   Was waiting to welcome you.
The branch bade you go,
   Where you tarried so long,
Where birds built a nest,
   Where they sang their sweet song.

As gently would I, when summer is done,
　Go at last to eternal rest;
I am told that God's heart is yearning for me,
　That there's room on His welcoming breast.
So why should I fear when a frost shall touch
　The stem that must set me free?
I shall go, please God, with a sweeter peace
　Than the leaf that fell from the tree.
　　　　　　　　—William M. Runyan

EVERY YEAR

The truer life draws nigher
　　　Every year.
And its morning star climbs higher
　　　Every year.
Earth's hold on us grows slighter,
And the heavy burden lighter,
And the dawn immortal brighter
　　　Every year.
　　　　　　　—Albert G. Pike

THE BIBLE

I hope in thy word—Psalm 119:81

BIBLE STUDY

Would it not be a foolish thing
To die of thirst, with this clear spring
Of living water at my feet?
To starve when there is bread and meat
And wine before me on the board,
A table spread by my dear Lord?
　　　　　　—Martha Snell Nicholson

God's Word

I paused last eve beside the blacksmith's door,
  And heard the anvil ring, the vesper's chime,
And looking in I saw upon the floor
  Old hammers, worn with beating years of time.
"How many anvils have you had?" said I,
  "To wear and batter all these hammers so?"
"Just one," he answered. Then with twinkling eye:
  "The anvil wears the hammers out, you know."
And so, I thought, the anvil of God's Word
  For ages skeptics' blows have beat upon,
But though the noise of falling blows was heard
  The anvil is unchanged; the hammers gone.
                              —*John Clifford*

From Miriam

We search the world for truth; we cull
The good, the true, the beautiful,
From graven stone and written scroll,
And all old flower-fields of the soul;
And, weary seekers of the best,
We come back laden from our quest,
To find that all the sages said
Is in the Book our mothers read.
                    —*John Greenleaf Whittier*

My Bible and I

We've traveled together,
  My Bible and I,
Through all kinds of weather,
  With smile or with sigh!
In sorrow or sunshine,
  In tempest or calm,

Thy friendship unchanging,
    My lamp and my psalm.

We've traveled together,
    My Bible and I,
When life had grown weary,
    And death e'en was nigh!
But all through the darkness
    Of mist or of wrong,
I found there a solace,
    A prayer, and a song.

So now who shall part us,
    My Bible and I?
Shall "isms" or schisms,
    Or "new lights" who try?
Shall shadow for substance,
    Or stone for good bread,
Supplant thy sound wisdom,
    Give folly instead?

Ah, no, my dear Bible,
    Exponent of light!
Thou sword of the spirit,
    Put error to flight!
And still through life's journey,
    Until my last sigh,
We'll travel together,
    My Bible and I.
                    —*Charles Sandford*

From THE CHRISTIAN YEAR

There is a book, who runs may read,
    Which heavenly truth imparts,
And all the lore its scholars need,
    Pure eyes and Christian hearts.
                    —*John Keble*

READING THE BOOK

Read then, but first thyself prepare
To read with zeal and mark with care;
And when thou read'st what here is writ
Let thy best practice second it:

So twice each precept read should be,
First in the Book and next in thee.

THE DIVINE VOLUME

Within that awful volume lies
The mystery of mysteries!
Happiest they of human race,
To whom their God has given grace
To read, to fear, to hope, to pray,
To lift the latch, to force the way;
But better had they ne'er been born,
That read to doubt, or read to scorn.
—*Walter Scott*

THE INCOMPARABLE TREASURE

Here is the Spring where waters flow,
    to quench our heat of sin:
Here is the Tree where truth does grow,
    to lead our lives therein:
Here is the Judge that stints the strife,
    when men's devices fail:
Here is the Bread that feeds the life,
    that death can not assail.
The tidings of Salvation dear,
    come to our ears from hence:
The fortress of our Faith is here,
    and shield of our defence.

Then be not like the hog, that has
  a pearl at his desire,
And takes more pleasure of the trough
  and wallowing in the mire.
Read not this book, in any case,
  but with a single eye:
Read not, but first desire God's grace,
  to understand thereby.
                    —(*From an Old Bible*)

THY WORD IS LIKE A GARDEN, LORD

Thy Word is like a garden, Lord,
  With flowers bright and fair;
And ev'ry one who seeks may pluck
  A lovely cluster there.
Thy Word is like a deep, deep mine,
  And jewels rich and rare
Are hidden in its mighty depths
  For ev'ry searcher there.

Thy Word is like a starry host:
  A thousand rays of light
Are seen to guard the traveler,
  And make his pathway bright.
Thy Word is like an armory,
  Where soldiers may repair,
And find, for life's long battleday,
  All needful weapons there.

Oh, may I love Thy precious Word,
  May I explore the mine,
May I its fragrant flowers glean,
  May light upon me shine!
Oh, may I find my armor there!
  Thy Word my trusty sword,

I'll learn to fight with every foe
The battle of the Lord.
—*T. H. Gill*

A BIT OF THE BOOK

A bit of the book in the morning,
To order my onward way.
A bit of the book in the evening,
To hallow the end of the day.
—*Margaret E. Sangster*

BIRTH OF CHRIST

For behold, I bring you good tidings of great joy, which shall be to all people. For unto you is born this day, in the city of David, a Saviour, which is Christ the Lord —*Luke 2:10, 11*

THE HOUSE OF CHRISTMAS

To an open house in the evening,
Home shall men come,
To an older place than Eden,
And a taller town than Rome.
To the end of the way of the wandering star,
To the things that cannot be and that are,
To the place where God was homeless,
And all men are at home.
—*G. K. Chesterton*

THERE'S A SONG IN THE AIR

There's a song in the air!
There's a star in the sky!

There's a mother's deep prayer,
    And a baby's low cry!
And the star rains its fire while the beautiful sing,
For the manger of Bethlehem cradles a King!

There's a tumult of joy
    O'er the wonderful birth,
For the Virgin's sweet boy
    Is the Lord of the earth.
Ay! the star rains its fire while the beautiful sing,
For the manager of Bethlehem cradles a King!

In the light of that star
    Lie the ages impearled;
And that song from afar
    Has swept over the world.
Every hearth is aflame, and the beautiful sing,
In the homes of the nations, that Jesus is King!

We rejoice in the light,
    And we echo the song
That comes down through the night
    From the heavenly throng.
Ay! we shout to the lovely evangel they bring,
And we greet in his cradle our Saviour and King!
                                   —*Josiah G. Holland*

WELCOME!

Welcome, all wonders in one sight!
    Eternity shut in a span.
Summer in winter. Day in night.
    Heaven in earth, and God in man.
Great little one! whose all-embracing birth
Lifts earth to heaven, stoops heav'n to earth. . . .

To thee, meek majesty! soft king
   Of simple graces and sweet loves,
Each of us his lamb will bring
   Each his pair of silver doves;
Till burnt at last in fire of thy fair eyes,
Our selves become our own best sacrifice.
                    —Richard Crashaw

HAIL, JESUS!

Hail, thou long-expected Jesus,
   Born to set thy people free,
From our sins and fears release us;
   Let us find our rest in thee.
Israel's strength and consolation,
   Hope of all the saints thou art;
Long desired of every nation,
   Joy of every waiting heart.

Born thy people to deliver,
   Born a child,—and yet a King,—
Born to reign in us forever,
   Now thy gracious kingdom bring.
By thine own eternal Spirit,
   Rule in all our hearts alone;
By thine all-sufficient merit,
   Raise us to thy glorious throne.
                    —Charles Wesley

COMMITMENT

Also I heard the voice of the Lord, saying,
Whom shall I send, and who will go for us?
Then said I, Here am I; send me—Isaiah 6:8

From SAINT PAUL

Whoso has felt the Spirit of the Highest
   Cannot confound nor doubt Him nor
     deny:
Yea, with one voice, O world, tho' thou
     deniest,
   Stand thou on that side, for on this
     am I.
       —Frederic W. H. Myers

MAKE ME THY FUEL

From prayer that asks that I may be
Sheltered from winds that beat on Thee,
From fearing when I should aspire,
From faltering when I should climb higher,
From silken self, O Captain, free
Thy soldier who would follow Thee.

From subtle love of softening things,
From easy choices, weakenings,
Not thus are spirits fortified,
Not this way went the Crucified,
From all that dims Thy Calvary,
O Lamb of God, deliver me.

Give me the love that leads the way,
The faith that nothing can dismay,
The hope no disappointments tire,
The passion that will burn like fire,
Let me not sink to be a clod:
Make me Thy fuel, Flame of God.

—Amy Carmichael

SACRIFICE

Lord, I have laid my heart upon Thy altar,
    But cannot get the wood to burn;
It hardly flares ere it begins to falter,
    And to the dark return.
Old sap, or night-fallen dew, has damped
        the fuel;
    In vain my breath would flame pro-
        voke;
Yet see—at every poor attempt's renewal
    To Thee ascends the smoke!
'Tis all I have—smoke, failure, foiled en-
        deavor,
    Coldness and doubt, and palsied lack:
Such as I have I send Thee; perfect Giver,
    Send Thou Thy lightning back!

—George Macdonald.

THE MASTER'S TOUCH

In the still air the music lies unheard;
    In the rough marble beauty hides unseen:
To make the music and the beauty, needs
    The master's touch, the sculptor's chisel keen.

Great Master, touch us with thy skillful hand;
    Let not the music that is in us die!

Great Sculptor, hew and polish us; nor let,
  Hidden and lost, thy form within us lie!

Spare not the stroke! do with us as thou wilt!
  Let there be naught unfinished, broken,
  marred;
Complete thy purpose, that we may become
  Thy perfect image, thou our God and Lord!
              —*Horatius Bonar*

TAKE MY LIFE

Take my life and let it be
Consecrated, Lord, to thee;
Take my moments and my days,
Let them flow in endless praise;
Take my hands and let them move
At the impulse of thy love;
Take my feet and let them be
Swift and beautiful for thee.

Take my voice and let me sing,
Always, only, for my King.
Take my lips and let them be
Filled with messages from thee.
Take my silver and my gold;
Not a mite would I withhold.
Take my intellect and use
Every power as thou shalt choose.

Take my will and make it thine;
It shall be no longer mine.
Take my heart, it is thine own;
It shall be thy royal throne.
Take my love, my Lord, I pour
At thy feet its treasure-store.

Take myself, and I will be
Ever, only, all for thee.
                    —*Frances Ridley Havergal*

CONCERN

Be kindly affectioned one to another with brotherly love, in honour
preferring one another   —*Romans 12:10*

AWARENESS

God—let me be aware.
Let me not stumble blindly down the ways,
Just getting somehow safely through the days,
Not even groping for another hand,
Not even wondering why it all was planned,
Eyes to the ground unseeking for the light,
Soul never aching for a wild-winged flight,
Please, keep me eager just to do my share.
God—let me be aware.

God—let me be aware.
Stab my soul fiercely with others' pain,
Let me walk seeing horror and stain.
Let my hands, groping, find other hands.
Give me the heart that divines, understands.
Give me the courage, wounded, to fight.
Flood me with knowledge, drench me in light.
Please, keep me eager just to do my share.
God—let me be aware.
                    —*Miriam Teichner*

From ANDREW RYKMAN'S PRAYER

If there be some weaker one,
Give me strength to help him on;

If a blinder soul there be,
Let me guide him nearer thee.
Make my mortal dreams come true
With the work I fain would do;
Clothe with life the weak intent,
Let me be the thing I meant;
Let me find in thy employ
Peace that dearer is than joy;
Out of self to love be led
And to heaven acclimated,
Until all things sweet and good
Seem my natural habitude.
                    —*John Greenleaf Whittier*

THE THING YOU LEAVE UNDONE

It isn't the thing you do, dear,
    It's the thing you leave undone,
Which gives you the bitter heartache
    At the setting of the sun;

The tender word unspoken,
    The letter you did not write,
The flower you might have sent, dear,
    Are your haunting ghosts at night.

The stone you might have lifted
    Out of your brother's way,
The bit of heartsome counsel
    You were hurried too much to say;
The loving touch of the hand, dear,
    The gentle and winsome tone,
That you had no time or thought for,
    With troubles enough of your own.

These little acts of kindness,
    So easily out of mind,

These chances to be angels,
   Which even mortals find—
They come in night and silence,
   Each chill reproachful wraith,
When hope is faint and flagging,
   And a blight has dropped on faith.

For life is all too short, dear.
   And sorrow is all too great,
To suffer our slow compassion
   That tarries until too late.
And it's not the thing you do, dear,
   It's the thing you leave undone,
Which gives you the bitter heartache,
   At the setting of the sun.
              —*Adelaide Procter*

MY DAILY CREED

Let me be a little kinder,
   Let me be a little blinder
To the faults of those about me;
   Let me praise a little more;
Let me be, when I am weary,
   Just a little bit more cheery;
Let me serve a little better
   Those that I am striving for.

Let me be a little braver
   When temptation bids me waver;
Let me strive a little harder
   To be all that I should be;
Let me be a little meeker
   With the brother that is weaker;
Let me think more of my neighbor
   And a little less of me.

I Shall Not Pass Again this Way

The bread that bringeth strength I want to give,
The water pure that bids the thirsty live;
I want to help the fainting day by day;
I'm sure I shall not pass again this way.

I want to give the oil of joy for tears,
The faith to conquer crowding doubts and fears,
Beauty for ashes may I give always;
I'm sure I shall not pass again this way.

I want to give good measure running o'er
And into angry hearts I want to pour
The answer soft that turneth wrath away;
I'm sure I shall not pass again this way.

I want to give to others hope and faith;
I want to do all that the Master saith;
I want to live aright from day to day;
I'm sure I shall not pass again this way.

—Ellen H. Underwood

DEATH AND LIFE ETERNAL

I am the resurrection, and the life—John 11:23

Emancipation

Why be afraid of death
As though your life were breath?
Death but anoints your eyes
With clay, O glad surprise!
Why should you be forlorn?
Death only husks the corn.
Why should you fear to meet
The Thresher of the wheat?

Is sleep a thing to dread?
Yet, sleeping you are dead
    Till you awake and rise,
    Here, or beyond the skies.
Why should it be a wrench
To leave your wooden bench?
    Why not, with happy shout,
    Run home when school is out?
The dear ones left behind?
O foolish one and blind,
    A day, and you will meet;
    A night, and you will greet.
This is the death of death:
To breathe away a breath,
    And know the end of strife,
    And taste the deathless life,
And joy without a fear,
And smile without a tear,
    And work, not care nor rest,
    And find the last the best.
            —Maltbie D. Babcock

DOMINION

Soft floods of moonlight,
Bare sweep of sky,
Black depths star sprinkled—
Yet beyond lie
Wonders unfathomed.
I, what am I?

Mystery and motion,
Roll of the sea,
Endless horizon,
Winds blowing free.
These serve creation,

Asking not why,
Yet my heart ponders,
I, what am I?

Sky, land or ocean,
Brief is your sway;
Vast reach of spaces,
Dwindle away!
These shall be nothing,
Earth, deep and sky—
Breath of God's nostrils,
Eternal am I!
      —Martha Snell Nicholson

THERE'S MORE

We only see a little of the ocean,
A few miles distance from the rocky shore;
But oh! out there beyond—beyond the eyes'
    horizon
  There's more—there's more.

We only see a little of God's loving,
A few rich treasures from his mighty store;
But oh! out there beyond—beyond our life's
    horizon
  There's more—there's more.

HIDDEN TREASURE

'Twas long ago I read the story sweet—
Of how the German mothers, o'er the sea,
Wind in, throughout the yarn their girlies
    knit,
Some trinkets small, and tiny shining
    coins,
That when the little fingers weary grow,

And fain would lay aside the tiresome
        task,
From out the ball will drop the hidden
        gift,
To please and urge them on in search
        for more.
And so, I think, the Father kind above
Winds in and out the skein of life we
        weave,
Through all the years, bright tokens of
        His love,
That when we weary grow and long for
        rest
They help to cheer and urge us on for
        more;
And far adown within the ball we find,
When all the threads of life at last are
        spun,
The grandest gift of all—eternal life.

LIFE AND DEATH

Frail Life! in which, through mists of human breath
We grope for truth, and make our progress slow,
Because by passion blinded; till, by death
Our passions ending, we begin to know.

O reverend Death! whose looks can soon advise
E'en scornful youth, while priests their doctrine waste;
Yet mocks us too; for he does make us wise,
When by his coming our affairs are past.

O harmless Death! whom still the valiant brave,
The wise expect, the sorrowful invite,
And all the good embrace, who know the grave
A short dark passage to eternal light.

                        —*William Davenant*

THE AUTHOR'S EPITAPH, MADE BY HIMSELF

Even such is Time, which takes in trust
Our youth, our joys, and all we have,
And pays us but with age and dust;
Who in the dark and silent grave,
When we have wandered all our ways,
Shuts up the story of our days:
And from which earth, and grave, and dust,
The Lord shall raise me up I trust.

—*Walter Raleigh*

L'ENVOI

O love triumphant over guilt and sin,
My soul is soiled, but Thou shalt enter in;
My feet must stumble if I walk alone,
Lonely my heart, till beating by Thine own,
My will is weakness till it rest in Thine,
Cut off, I wither, thirsting for the Vine,
My deeds are dry leaves on a sapless tree,
My life is lifeless till it live in Thee!

—*Frederic Lawrence Knowles*

DEATH

Death, be not proud, though some have called thee
Mighty and dreadful, for thou art not so:
For those whom thou think'st thou dost overthrow
Die not, poor Death; nor yet canst thou kill me.
From Rest and Sleep, which but thy picture be,
Much pleasure, then from thee much more must flow;
And soonest our best men with thee do go—
Rest of their bones and souls' delivery!
Thou'rt slave to fate, chance, kings, and desperate men,
And dost with poison, war, and sickness dwell;

And poppy or charms can make us sleep as well
And better than thy stroke. Why swell'st thou then?
    One short sleep past, we wake eternally,
    And Death shall be no more: Death, thou shalt die!
                    —John Donne

FAITH

*Now faith is the substance of things hoped for,
the evidence of things not seen—Hebrews 11:1*

THE THREAD AND THE CABLE

Though waves and billows o'er me pass
    In whelming floods of ill,
Within the haven of God's love
    My soul is anchored still;
For though the stress and strain of life
    My thread of faith may break,
The cable of His faithfulness
    No storm can ever shake.
             —Annie Johnson Flint

OVERHEARD IN AN ORCHARD

Said the Robin to the Sparrow:
    "I should really like to know
Why these anxious human beings
    Rush about and worry so?"

Said the Sparrow to the Robin:
    "Friend, I think that it must be
That they have no heavenly Father
    Such as cares for you and me."
             —Elizabeth Cheney

HOPE

Great God of Hope, how green Thy trees,
    How calm each several star.
Renew us; make us fresh as these,
    Calm as those are.

For what can dim his hope who sees,
    Though faintly and afar,
The power that kindles green in trees,
    And light in star?

—*Amy Carmichael*

PEACE

When winds are raging o'er the upper ocean,
    And billows wild contend with angry roar,
'Tis said, far down beneath the wild commotion,
    That peaceful stillness reigneth evermore.

Far, far beneath, the noise of tempest dieth,
    And silver waves chime ever peacefully,
And no rude storm, how fierce soe'er it flieth,
    Disturbs the Sabbath of that deeper sea.

So to the heart that knows Thy love, O Purest,
    There is a temple sacred evermore,
And all the babble of life's angry voices
    Dies in hushed silence at its peaceful door.

Far, far away, the roar of passion dieth,
    And loving thoughts rise calm and peacefully,
And no rude storm, how fierce soe'er it flieth,
    Disturbs the soul that dwells, O Lord, in Thee.

—*Harriet Beecher Stowe*

THE EVIDENCE

In every seed to breathe the flower,
    In every drop of dew

To reverence a cloistered star
Within the distant blue;
To wait the promise of the bow
Despite the cloud between,
Is Faith—the fervid evidence
Of loveliness unseen.

—John Banister Tabb

I NEED THEE

My Lord, I have no clothes to come to thee;
My shoes are pierced and broken with the road;
I am torn and weathered, wounded with the goad,
And soiled with tugging at my weary load:
The more I need thee! A very prodigal
I stagger into thy presence, Lord of me:
One look, my Christ, and at thy feet I fall!

—George Macdonald

CONFIDENCE

Thou layest Thy hand on the fluttering heart
   And sayest, "Be still!"
The shadow and silence are only a part
   Of Thy sweet will.
Thy Presence is with me, and where Thou art
   I fear no ill.

—Frances Ridley Havergal

FAITH

God knows, not I, the reason why
   His winds of storm drive through my door;
I am content to live or die
   Just knowing this, nor knowing more.

My Father's hand appointing me
My days and ways, so I am free.
                    —*Margaret E. Sangster*

FAITH AND SIGHT

So I go on, not knowing,—
    I would not, if I might—
I would rather walk in the dark with God
    Than go alone in the light;
I would rather walk with Him by faith
    Than walk alone by sight.
                    —*Mary Gardner Brainard*

LEAN HARD

Child of My love, lean hard,
And let Me feel the pressure of thy care;
I know thy burden, child. I shaped it;
Poised it in Mine Own hand; made no proportion
In its weight to thine unaided strength,
For even as I laid it on, I said,
"I shall be near, and while she leans on Me,
This burden shall be Mine, not hers;
So shall I keep My child within the circling arms
Of My Own love." Here lay it down, nor fear
To impose it on a shoulder which upholds
The government of worlds. Yet closer come:
Thou art not near enough. I would embrace thy care;
So I might feel My child reposing on My breast.
Thou lovest Me? I knew it. Doubt not then;
But loving Me, lean hard.

BE STILL

Dear restless heart, be still; don't fret and worry so;
God has a thousand ways His love and help to show;
Just trust, and trust, and trust, until His will you know.

Dear restless heart, be still, for peace is God's own smile,
His love can every wrong and sorrow reconcile;
Just love, and love, and love, and calmly wait awhile.

Dear restless heart, be brave; don't moan and sorrow so,
He hath a meaning kind in chilly winds that blow;
Just hope, and hope, and hope, until you braver grow.

Dear restless heart, repose upon His breast this hour,
His grace is strength and life, His love is bloom and flower;
Just rest, and rest, and rest, within His tender power.

Dear restless heart, be still! Don't struggle to be free;
God's life is in your life, from Him you may not flee;
Just pray, and pray, and pray, till you have faith to see.

—Edith Willis Linn

FELLOWSHIP

*God is faithful, by whom ye were called unto the
fellowship of his Son Jesus Christ our Lord*
—I Corinthians 1:9

PRAYER IN A JUNE GARDEN

Dear God, Your roses bloom so very sweetly—
Your shadows lie so softly on the grass!
The very singing winds that try to pass
Must linger in this lovely place . . .
    Completely
Your presence here is felt, this tender garden
Is all Your Own, each fragrant flower head
Is rising like Your voice. Each mossy bed
Is like a psalm that breathes of peace and pardon.

Dear Father, You, Who made the tender showers,
Who made the sunlight coming after rain,
Have made new hope, to follow after pain!

Life must be formed of alternating hours,
Some fair, some dim . . . some wonderful with grace . . .
We, who are pilgrims, only ask You this—
That we may know, at times, the utter bliss
Of walking with You, in some garden place.

—Amen

BEGIN THE DAY WITH GOD

Begin the day with God!
  He is thy Sun and Day!
His is the radiance of thy dawn;
  To Him address thy lay.

Sing a new song at morn!
  Join the glad woods and hills;
Join the fresh winds and seas and plains,
  Join the bright flowers and rills.

Sing thy first song to God!
  Not to thy fellow men;
Not to the creatures of His hand,
  But to the glorious One.

Take thy first walk with God!
  Let Him go forth with thee;
By stream, or sea, or mountain path,
  Seek still His company.

Thy first transaction be
  With God Himself above;
So shall thy business prosper well,
  And all the day be love.

—Horatius Bonar

TO MY GOD

Oh how oft I wake and find
  I have been forgetting thee!

I am never from thy mind:
Thou it is that wakest me.
—*George Macdonald*

THE HEART'S COUNTRY

Hill people turn to their hills;
    Sea-folk are sick for the sea:
Thou art my land and my country,
    And my heart calls out for thee.

The bird beats his wings for the open,
    The captive burns to be free;
But I—I cry at thy window,
    For thou art my liberty.
—*Florence Wilkinson*

I LOVE MY GOD

I love my God, but with no love of mine,
    For I have none to give;
I love Thee, Lord; but all the love is Thine,
    For by Thy life I live.
I am as nothing, and rejoice to be
Emptied, and lost, and swallowed up in Thee.

Thou, Lord, alone, art all Thy childen need,
    And there is none beside;
From Thee the streams of blessedness proceed,
    In Thee the blest abide,—
Fountain of life, and all-abounding grace,
Our source, our center, and our dwelling-place.
—*Jeanne Marie Guyon*

THE LORD OF JOY

Ye that do your Master's will,
Meek in heart be meeker still:

Day by day your sins confess,
Ye that walk in righteousness:
Gracious souls in grace abound,
Seek the Lord, whom ye have found.

He that comforts all that mourn
Shall to joy your sorrow turn:
Joy to know your sins forgiven,
Joy to keep the way to heaven,
Joy to win His welcome grace,
Joy to see Him face to face.

—Charles Wesley

THE GOLDEN CORD

Through every minute of this day,
    Be with me, Lord!
Through every day of all this week,
    Be with me, Lord!
Through every week of all this year,
    Be with me, Lord!
Through all the years of all this life,
    Be with me, Lord!
So shall the days and weeks and years
Be threaded on a golden cord,
And all draw on with sweet accord
Unto Thy fulness, Lord,
That so, when time is past,
By Grace, I may at last
    Be with Thee, Lord.

—John Oxenham

GROWTH

But grow in grace, and in the knowledge of our Lord
and Saviour Jesus Christ   —II Peter 3:18

HIGHER GROUND

I'm pressing on the upward way,
New heights I'm gaining every day;
Still praying as I'm onward bound,
"Lord, plant my feet on higher ground."

Lord, lift me up and let me stand,
By faith, on heaven's tableland,
A higher plane than I have found;
Lord, plant my feet on higher ground.

My heart has no desire to stay
Where doubts arise and fears dismay;
Though some may dwell where these abound,
My prayer, my aim, is higher ground.

I want to live above the world,
Though Satan's darts at me are hurled;
For faith has caught the joyful sound,
The song of saints on higher ground.

I want to scale the utmost height,
And catch a gleam of glory bright;
But still I'll pray till heaven I've found,
"Lord, lead me on to higher ground."

                    —Johnson Oatman, Jr.

THE MOUNT OF BLESSING

He went into a mountain . . . his disciples came unto him.
—Matthew 6:1

I never can rest when hills are before me,
   Their purples and grays seem as voices that call;
The pines on their crests are like arms that implore me;
   Their majesty pleads, and their glories enthrall.
I never can rest when the hills, standing high,
Give lure to my feet to push on toward the sky.

O Soul, why at ease, when summits are calling
   Where holy beatitudes sweeten the air?
Thy sandals close bind, let thy footsteps be falling
   On heights of communion, of praise and of prayer.
O Soul, why at ease? On the mount with the King
Are the vistas and voices that thrill and that sing.

—William M. Runyan

THE SECRETS OF LIFE

We would miss the fleecy vapor,
If the skies were always blue
We would miss the pearly sparkles
If there never was a dew;
We would long for shade and darkness
Were the hours like brightest day;
We would sigh for hills and valleys
Were our path a level way.

Thus it is on life's brief journey—
There must be both night and day;

There must come the rain and sunshine,
On our rough uneven way;
There must be some days of sorrow,
Where the heart is crushed with grief,
When the tears will flow in silence,
And their falling brings relief.

We must learn life's secret lesson—
Blending bitter with the sweet,
Sending sunshine with the raindrops
Bringing to us cold and heat.
We must learn the art of blending;
We must needs pass through the deep
Ever pressing onward, forward,
Till we climb the mountains steep.
                              —N. P. Neilson

THE LAST DEFILE

"He died climbing"—A Swiss Guide's Epitaph

Make us Thy mountaineers:
We would not linger on the lower slope,
Fill us afresh with hope, O God of Hope,
That undefeated we may climb the hill
As seeing Him who is invisible.

Let us die climbing. When this little while
Lies far behind us, and the last defile
Is all alight, and in that light we see
Our Leader and our Lord, what will it be?
                              —Amy Carmichael

LOST AND FOUND

I missed him when the sun began to bend;
I found him not when I had lost his rim;

With many tears I went in search of him,
Climbing high mountains which did still ascend,
And gave me echoes when I called my friend;
Through cities vast and charnel-houses grim,
And high cathedrals where the light was dim,
Through books and arts and works without an end,
But found him not—the friend whom I had lost.
And yet I found him—as I found the lark,
A sound in fields I heard but could not mark;
I found him in my heart, a life in frost,
A light I knew not till my soul was dark.

—*George Macdonald*

GUIDANCE

He leadeth me beside the still waters—Psalm 23:2

From THE GATE OF THE YEAR

And I said to the man who stood at the gate of the year:
"Give me a light, that I may tread safely into the unknown!"
And he replied:
"Go out into the darkness and put thine hand into the Hand of God.
That shall be to thee better than light and safer than a known way."
So, I went forth, and finding the Hand of God, trod gladly into the
    night.

—*Minnie Louise Haskins*

HE UPHOLDS

For who that leans on His right arm
    Was ever yet forsaken?

What righteous cause can suffer harm
 If He its part has taken?
  Though wild and loud
  And dark the cloud,
  Behind its folds
  His hand upholds
 The calm sky of to-morrow.
     —*Martin Luther*

REST ON HIM

He who hath led will lead
 All through the wilderness;
He who hath fed will feed;
 He who hath blessed will bless;
He who hath heard thy cry
 Will never close His ear;
He who hath marked thy faintest sigh
 Will not forget thy tear.
He loveth always, faileth never;
So rest on Him to-day, forever.
    —*Frances Ridley Havergal*

HIS HAND

The Hand that binds the star
 To its far centre, and around it rolls
Through space its worlds, with never halt nor jar,
 No less my steps controls.

That same unfailing Hand
 Hath led me forth from still eternity;
'Twill guide me onward through star-vistas, and
 I follow trustingly.
    —*Henry Jerome Stockard*

THE DAY—THE WAY

Not for one single day
Can I discern my way,
    But this I surely know,—
Who gives the day
Will show the way,
    So I securely go.
          —*John Oxenham*

HIS WAY

Who walks with God must take His way,
Across far distances and gray,
To goals that others do not see,
Where others do not care to be.

Who walks with God must have no fear
When danger and defeat appear,
Nor stop when every hope seems gone,
For God, our God, moves ever on.

Who walks with God must press ahead
When sun or cloud is overhead,
When all the waiting thousands cheer,
Or when they only stop to sneer;

When all the challenge leaves the hours
And naught is left but jaded powers;
But he will some day reach the dawn,
For God, our God, moves ever on.

THE LORD'S MY SHEPHERD

The Lord's my shepherd; I'll not want;
    He makes me down to lie
In pastures green: He leadeth me
    The quiet waters by.

My soul He doth restore again;
    And me to walk doth make
Within the paths of righteousness,
    E'en for His own name's sake.

Yea, though I walk in death's dark vale,
    Yet will I fear no ill;
For Thou art with me: and Thy rod
    And staff me comfort still.

My table Thou hast furnished
    In presence of my foes;
My head Thou dost with oil anoint,
    And my cup overflows.

Goodness and mercy all my life
    Shall surely follow me;
And in God's house forever more
    My dwelling-place shall be.

                    —*Psalm 23*

UP-HILL

Does the road wind up-hill all the way?
    Yes, to the very end.
Will the day's journey take the whole long day?
    From morn to night, my friend.

But is there for the night a resting-place?
    A roof for when the slow dark hours begin.
May not the darkness hide it from my face?
    You cannot miss that inn.

Shall I meet other wayfarers at night?
    Those who have gone before.
Then must I knock, or call when just in sight?
    They will not keep you standing at that door.

Shall I find comfort, travel-sore and weak?
    Of labour you shall find the sum.

Will there be beds for me and all who seek?
Yes, beds for all who come.

—Christina Rossetti

LIGHT SHINING OUT OF DARKNESS

God moves in a mysterious way
    His wonders to perform;
He plants his footsteps in the sea,
    And rides upon the storm.

Deep in unfathomable mines
    Of never-failing skill,
He treasures up his bright designs
    And works his sovereign will.

Ye fearful saints, fresh courage take,
    The clouds ye so much dread
Are big with mercy, and shall break
    In blessings on your head.

Judge not the Lord by feeble sense,
    But trust him for his grace;
Behind a frowning providence
    He hides a smiling face.

His purposes will ripen fast,
    Unfolding every hour;
The bud may have a bitter taste,
    But sweet will be the flower.

Blind unbelief is sure to err,
    And scan his work in vain:
God is his own interpreter,
    And he will make it plain.

—William Cowper

LEAD ME

I do not ask, O Lord, that Thou shouldst shed
  Full radiance here:
Give but a ray of peace, that I may tread
  Without a fear.
I do not ask my cross to understand,
  My way to see—
Better in darkness just to feel Thy hand
  And follow Thee.
Joy is like restless day, but peace divine
  Like quiet night;
Lead me, O Lord, till perfect day shall shine,
  Through Peace to Light.
                    —*Adelaide A. Procter*

THE BLESSED JOURNEY

Let Him lead thee blindfold onwards,
  Love needs not to know;
Children whom the Father leadeth
  Ask not where they go.
Though the path be all unknown,
Over moors and mountains lone.

Give no ear to reason's questions;
  Let the blind man hold
That the sun is but a fable
  Men believed of old.
At the breast the babe will grow;
Whence the milk he need not know.
                    —*Gerhard Tersteegen*

GOD'S WAY

Thy way, not mine, O Lord!
  However dark it be;

Lead me by Thine own hand,
    Choose out the path for me.

Smooth let it be, or rough,
    It will be still the best;
Winding or straight it matters not,
    It leads me to Thy rest.

I dare not choose my lot,
    I would not, if I might;
Choose Thou for me, O God!
    So shall I walk aright.

The kingdom that I seek
    Is Thine; so let the way
That leads to it be Thine;
    Else I must surely stray.

Take Thou my cup, and it
    With joy or sorrow fill;
As best to Thee may seem;
    Choose Thou my good or ill.

Not mine, not mine the choice
    In things or great or small;
Be Thou my guide, my strength,
    My wisdom and my all.
                  —*Horatius Bonar*

AT THE PLACE OF THE SEA

"By the greatness of thine arm they shall be still . . . till thy people pass over, O Lord"   —*Exodus 15:16*

Have you come to the Red Sea place in your life,
    Where, in spite of all you can do,
There is no way out, there is no way back,
    There is no other way but—through?

Then wait on the Lord with a trust serene
    Till the night of your fear is gone;
He will send the wind, He will heap the floods,
    When He says to your soul, "Go on."

And His hand will lead you through—clear through—
    Ere the watery walls roll down,
No foe can reach you, no wave can touch,
    No mightiest sea can drown;
The tossing billows may rear their crests,
    Their foam at your feet may break,
But over their bed you shall walk dry shod
    In the path that your Lord will make.

In the morning watch, 'neath the lifted cloud,
    You shall see but the Lord alone,
When He leads you on from the place of the sea
    To land that you have not known;
And your fears shall pass as your foes have passed,
    You shall be no more afraid;
You shall sing His praise in a better place,
    A place that His hand has made.
                        —*Annie Johnson Flint*

HEAVEN

*For I am in a strait betwixt two, having a desire to depart,
and to be with Christ, which is far better*
                        —*Philippians 1:23*

DEATH

Christ leads me through no darker rooms
Than he went through before;
He that unto God's kingdom comes,
Must enter by this door. . . .

My knowledge of that life is small,
The eye of faith is dim;
But 'tis enough that Christ knows all,
And I shall be with him.

—*Richard Baxter*

The Upper Road

I'm going by the upper road, for that
        still holds the sun,
I'm climbing through night's pastures where
        the starry rivers run:
If you should think to seek me in my
        old dark abode,
You'll find this writing on the door,
        "He's on the Upper Road."

With Him

There no more parting, no more pain
    The distant ones brought near,
The lost so long are found again,
    Long lost but longer dear:
Eye hath not seen, ear hath not heard,
    Nor heart conceived that rest,
With them our good things long deferred,
    With Jesus Christ our Best.

—*Christina Rossetti*

Dying

What is it like, this dying?
Soul, it is wings, and flying,

Light, and an end of groping,
End of the heart's deep hoping,

End of the spirit's longing,
Dreams come true in the dawning!

Living—I taste God's grace;
Dying—I see His face!
        —*Martha Snell Nicholson*

WE'LL MEET THEM

And those dear loved of ours we miss so sorely,
    Do they not, too, all glad, expectant, wait?
Till down the steeps of light, athrob with glory,
    They'll throng—that shining host—from Heaven's gate!

We'll meet them in that Resurrection morning!
    We'll find each dear, familiar, longed-for face;
We'll know them e'en though radiant and transfigured;
    Once more we'll clasp our own—oh, gift of grace!
                —*Mrs. Donald A. Day*

THE SYMPHONY

O sound the grand symphony down through the years!
The ages are climbing away from their biers!
Christ came, by the portal—mortality's womb—
And opened, towards heaven, the gates of the tomb!
There's a tidal uplifting—hope cleaving—faith hears
The building of mansions, for us, in the spheres!
                —*Charlotte Grant MacIntyre*

TWO HOMES

A friend sent me the other day
A picture of her home.
It seemed a palace to my eyes,
With porticos and dome,

And windows flashing in the sun.
She says words cannot tell

The beauty of its furnishings.
A lordly place to dwell!

And yet I grieve because it is
The only home she has,
And when it feels the touch of time
It will decay and pass.

While I, although my earthly home
Is but a cottage small,
Have never tasted poverty
Nor any lack at all.

For on a distant, shining shore,
O fair, O lovely Land,
There waits for me another home
Which shall forever stand

When all the palaces of kings
Have crumbled into dust,
Betrayed by every brick and stone
In which they put their trust.

Untouched by time the mansion planned
By Architect divine!
The nail-pierced hands of my dear Lord
Have built that home of mine!
                    —*Martha Snell Nicholson*

OUT OF THE HEAT

Out of the heat and out of the rain,
Never to know or sin or pain,
Never to fall and never to fear,
Could we wish better for one so dear?

What has he seen and what has he heard,
He who has flown away like a bird?
Eye has not seen, nor dream can show,
All he has seen, all he may know.

For the pure powers of Calvary
Bathe little souls in innocency;
Tender, tender Thy love-words be,
"Dear little child, come home to Me."
                    —*Amy Carmichael*

O HAPPY SOUL

O happy soul, be thankful now, and rest!
    Heaven is a goodly land;
And God is love; and those he loves are blest;
    Now thou dost understand
The least thou hast is better than the best
That thou didst hope for; now upon thine eyes
    The new life opens fair;
Before thy feet the blessed journey lies
    Through homelands everywhere;
And heaven to thee is all a sweet surprise.
                    —*Washington Gladden*

GOD'S ETERNAL NOW

Stillness midst the ever-changing,
    Lord, my rest art Thou;
So for me has dawned the morning,
    God's eternal NOW.
Now for me the day unsetting,
    Now the song begun;
Now, the deep surpassing glory,
    Brighter than the sun.

Hail! all hail! thou peaceful country
    Of eternal calm;
Summer land of milk and honey,
    Where the streams are balm.
There the Lord my Shepherd leads me,
    Wheresoe'er He will;

In the fresh green pastures feeds me,
   By the waters still.

Well I know them, those still waters!
   Peace and rest at last;
In their depths the quiet heavens
   Tell the storms are past,
Nought to mar the picture fair,
Of the glory resting there.
                    —*Gerhard Tersteegen*

HARVEST HOME

Out of the strain of the Doing
Into the peace of the Done
Out of the thirst of Pursuing
Into the rapture of Won
Out of grey mist into brightness
Out of pale dusk into Dawn—
Out of all wrong into rightness,
We from these fields shall be gone.
"Nay" say the saints "Not gone but come,
Into Eternity's Harvest Home."
                    —*W. M. L. Fay*

HOLINESS

Give unto the Lord the glory due unto his name;
worship the Lord in the beauty of holiness
                    —*Psalm 29:2*

UPON MY HEART

O for a heart to praise my God,
   A heart from sin set free!
A heart that's sprinkled with the blood
   So freely shed for me;

A heart resigned, submissive, meek,
   My dear Redeemer's throne,
Where only Christ is heard to speak,
   Where Jesus reigns alone;

An humble, lowly, contrite heart,
   Believing, true, and clean;
Which neither life nor death can part
   From him that dwells within.

A heart in every thought renewed,
   And full of love divine,
Perfect, and right, and pure, and good,
   A copy, Lord, of thine!

Thy nature, gracious Lord, impart;
   Come quickly from above;
Write thy new Name upon my heart,
   Thy new, best name of Love.
          —*Charles Wesley*

The Bird with a Broken Wing

I walked through the woodland meadows,
   Where sweet the thrushes sing,
And found on a bed of mosses
   A bird with a broken wing.
I healed its wound, and each morning
   It sang its old sweet strain;
But the bird with a broken pinion
   Never soared as high again.

I found a young life broken
   By sin's seductive art;
And, touched with a Christlike pity,
   I took him to my heart.
He lived with a noble purpose,
   And struggled not in vain;

But the life that sin had stricken
  Never soared as high again.

But the bird with a broken pinion
  Kept another from the snare,
And the life that sin had stricken
  Raised another from despair.
Each loss has its compensation,
  There is healing for every pain;
But the bird with a broken pinion
  Never soars as high again.
                    —*Hezekiah Butterworth*

God, Who Touchest Earth with Beauty

God, who touchest earth with beauty,
  Make my heart anew;
With thy Spirit re-create me,
  Pure, and strong, and true.

Like thy springs and running waters,
  Make me crystal pure;
Like thy rocks of towering grandeur,
  Make me strong and sure.

Like thy dancing waves in sunlight,
  Make me glad and free;
Like the straightness of the pine trees
  Let me upright be.

Like the arching of the heavens
  Lift my thoughts above,
Turn my dreams to noble action—
  Ministries of love.

Like the birds that soar while singing,
  Give my heart a song.
May the music of thanksgiving
  Echo clear and strong.

God, who touchest earth with beauty,
Make my heart anew;
Keep me ever by thy Spirit,
Pure, and strong, and true.
                    —*Mary S. Edgar*

A Clean Wind Blowing

God, keep a clean wind blowing through my heart,
Night and Day,
Cleanse it with sunlight, let the silver rain
Wash away
Cobwebs and the smouldering dust that years
Leave, I pray.
Bitterness can have no place in me,
Nor grief stay,
When the winds of God sweep through and wash
Them away.
God, keep a clean wind blowing through my heart
Night and day.

Make Us Thine

O King, enthroned on high,
Thou Comforter divine,
Blest Spirit of all truth, be nigh
And make us thine.

Thou art the Source of life,
Thou art our treasure-store;
Give us thy peace, and end our strife
For evermore.

Descend, O heavenly Dove,
Abide with us alway;
And in the fullness of thy love
Cleanse us, we pray.

For Thee

Search out in me all hidden sin,
And may Thy purity within
So cleanse my life, that it may be
A temple wholly fit for Thee.

Oh, search my life, my will, my all,
As now on Thee, my Lord, I call;
Purge me from self, and sanctify
My life, while Thee I glorify.

HOME

Now Jesus loved Martha, and her sister, and Lazarus—John 11:5

Home Dedication

We build an altar here, and pray
   That thou wilt show thy face;
Dear Lord, if thou wilt come to stay,
This home we consecrate today
   Will be a holy place.

Prayer for a New House

May our home be
A hearth-fire glowing bright,
A candle's mellow gleam,
A beacon in the night.

May our home give
Shelter to Thy poor.

Send wayfaring feet
To our open door.

May our home be
A signpost on the road—
May every pilgrim see
An altar raised to God!
—*Martha Snell Nicholson*

HOME

Home is a temple when the prayer
Of a humble heart is lifted there.
Home is a sanctuary, too,
Earth's dear retreat when the storms sweep through.
Home is a citadel of light
Against the dark unfriendly night,
Home is a haven, blest and fair—
All these, and more, if God is there.
—*Sybil Leonard Armes*

THE HOUSEWIFE

Jesus, teach me how to be
Proud of my simplicity.

Sweep the floors, wash the clothes,
Gather for each vase a rose.

Iron and tend a tiny frock,
Keeping one eye on the clock.

Always having time kept free
For childish questions asked of me.

Grant me wisdom Mary had
When she taught her little Lad.
—*Catherine Cate Coblentz*

O HAPPY HOME

O happy home, where Thou art loved the dearest,
  Thou loving Friend and Saviour of our race,
And where among the guests there never cometh,
  One who can hold such high and honored place.

O happy home, where Thou art not forgotten
  When joy is overflowing full and free;
O happy home, where every wounded spirit
  Is brought, Physician, Comforter, to Thee.
                              —*Carl J. P. Spitta*

ALTARS RAISED TO GOD

Who builds a home has made a wondrous thing,
A place for something more than sheltering.

These walls which reach toward God are housing life!
Unto this hearth a man may bring his wife,

Beneath this roof a child be born. How fine
The daily sacrament of bread and wine,

How clear the sunlight through the open door,
The leafy shadows patterned on the floor;

How sweet the hours of candle light, how deep
The peace which broods where little children sleep.

Throughout this whole land of ours how good
If all our homes were altars raised to God!
                              —*Martha Snell Nicholson*

JESUS CHRIST

*Wherefore God also hath highly exalted him, and given
him a name which is above every name, that at the name
of Jesus every knee should bow   —Philippians 2:9,10*

THAT HOLY THING

They all were looking for a king
    To slay their foes, and lift them high:
Thou cam'st a little baby thing
    That made a woman cry.

O son of man, to right my lot
    Nought but thy presence can avail;
Yet on the road thy wheels are not,
    Nor on the sea thy sail!

My fancied ways why shouldst thou heed?
    Thou com'st down thine own secret stair;
Com'st down to answer all my need,
    Yea, every bygone prayer!
                    —*George Macdonald*

THOU THYSELF

Lord, grant us eyes to see, and ears to hear,
    And souls to love, and minds to understand,
    And steadfast faces towards the Holy Land,
And confidence of hope, and filial fear,
And citizenship where Thy saints appear
    Before Thee heart in heart and hand in hand,
    And alleluias where their chanting band

As waters and as thunders fill the sphere.
Lord, grant us what Thou wilt, and what Thou wilt
Deny, and fold us in Thy peaceful fold:
   Not as the world gives, give to us Thine own:
Inbuild us where Jerusalem is built
With walls of jasper and with streets of gold,
   And Thou, Thyself, Lord Christ, for cornerstone.
                  —*Christina Rossetti*

CHRIST

He is a path, if any be misled;
   He is a robe, if any naked be;
If any chance to hunger, He is bread;
   If any be a bondman He is free;
   If any be but weak, how strong is He!
To dead men life He is, to sick men health;
To blind men sight, and to the needy wealth;
A pleasure without loss, a treasure without stealth.
                  —*Giles Fletcher*

THE MIDDLE-TIME

Between the exhilaration of Beginning . . .
   And the satisfaction of Concluding,
     Is the Middle-Time
        of Enduring . . . Changing . . . Trying . . .
           Despairing . . . Continuing . . . Becoming.

Jesus Christ was the Man of God's Middle-Time
   Between Creation and . . . Accomplishment.
Through him God said of Creation,
   "Without mistake."
And of Accomplishment,
   "Without doubt."

And we in our Middle-Times
  of Wondering and Waiting,
    Hurrying and Hesitating,
    Regretting and Revising—
We who have begun many things . . .
  and seen but few completed—
We who are becoming more . . . and less—
Through the evidence of God's Middle-Time

  Have a stabilizing hint
      That we are not mistakes,
      That we are irreplaceable,
      That our Being is of interest,
        and our Doing is of purpose,
      That our Being and our Doing
        are surrounded by *Amen*.

Jesus Christ is the Completer
  of unfinished people
  with unfinished work
  in unfinished times.

May he keep us from sinking, from ceasing,
  from wasting, from solidifying,
That we may be for him
  Experimenters, Enablers, Encouragers,
  and Associates in Accomplishment.
              —*Lona M. Fowler*

OUR BURDEN BEARER

The little sharp vexations
  And the briars that catch and fret,
Why not take all to the Helper
  Who has never failed us yet?

Tell Him about the heartache,
  And tell Him the longings, too;

Tell Him the baffled purpose
  When we scarce know what to do,

Then, leaving all our weakness
  With the One divinely strong,
Forget that we bore the burden,
  And carry away the song.
                    —*Phillips Brooks*

THY LOVE ALONE

Jesus, Thy love alone, alone Thy love,
        Refresheth me;
And for that love of Thine, that freshening love,
        I come to Thee.

It is Thy joy alone, alone Thy joy,
        That gladdens me;
And for that joy of Thine, that gladdening joy,
        I come to Thee.

Saviour, 'tis Thou Thyself, alone Thyself,
        Art all to me;
And for that all, of everything I need,
        I come to Thee.
                    —*Horatius Bonar*

COME VISIT US

Dear Friend, whose presence in the house,
  Whose gracious word benign,
Could once at Cana's wedding feast
  Turn water into wine,

Come visit us, and when dull work
  Grows weary, line on line,
Revive our souls, and make us see
  Life's water glow as wine.

Gay mirth shall deepen into joy,
   Earth's hopes shall grow divine,
When Jesus visits us, to turn
   Life's water into wine.
           —*James Freeman Clarke*

FAIREST LORD JESUS

Fairest Lord Jesus,
   Ruler of all nature,
O thou of God and man the Son;
   Thee will I cherish, thee will I honour,
Thou, my soul's glory, joy, and crown.

Fair are the meadows,
   Fairer still the woodlands,
Robed in the blooming garb of spring:
   Jesus is fairer, Jesus is purer,
Who makes the woeful heart to sing.

Fair is the sunshine,
   Fairer still the moonlight,
And all the twinkling, starry host:
   Jesus shines brighter, Jesus shines purer,
Than all the angels heaven can boast.

MISSIONS

*. . . and ye shall be witnesses unto me . . . unto the
uttermost part of the earth*   —*Acts 1:8*

SEND ME

Use me, God, in Thy great harvest field,
Which stretcheth far and wide like a wide sea;
The gatherers are so few; I fear the precious yield

Will suffer loss. Oh, find a place for me!
A place where best the strength I have will tell:
It may be one the older toilers shun;
Be it a wide or narrow place, 'tis well
So that the work it holds be only done.

—*Christina Rossetti*

From BEHOLD, THE FIELDS ARE WHITE

Where prophets' word, and martyrs' blood,
    And prayers of saints were sown,
We, to their labors entering in,
    Would reap where they have strown.

O thou whose call our hearts has stirred!
    To do thy will we come;
Thrust in our sickles at thy word,
    And bear our harvest home.

—*Samuel Longfellow*

STIR US, OH, STIR US, LORD

Stir us, oh, stir us, Lord, we care not how,
But stir our hearts in passion for the world;
Stir us to give, to go, but most to pray;
Stir till the blood-red banner be unfurled
O'er lands that still in heathen darkness lie,
O'er deserts where no Cross is lifted high.

THE MISSIONARIES

O missionaries of the Blood! Ambassadors of God!
Our souls flame in us when we see where ye have fearless trod
At break of day; your dauntless faith our slackened valor shames,
And every eve our joyful prayers are jeweled with your names.

—*Robert McIntyre*

IN SPITE OF SORROW

In spite of sorrow, loss, and pain,
   Our course be onward still;
We sow on Burmah's barren plain,
   We reap on Zion's hill.
               —Adoniram Judson

KING TRIUMPHANT

Jesus shall reign where'er the sun
   Does his successive journeys run;
His kingdom spread from shore to shore,
   Till moons shall wax and wane no more.

From north to south the princes meet,
   To pay their homage at his feet;
While western empires own their Lord,
   And savage tribes attend his word.

To him shall endless prayer be made,
   And endless praises crown his head;
His name, like sweet perfume, shall rise
   With ev'ry morning sacrifice.

People and realms of ev'ry tongue
   Dwell on his love with sweetest song,
And infant voices shall proclaim
   Their early blessings on his name.
               —Isaac Watts

THE NEW BIRTH

Being born again, not of corruptible seed, but of incorruptible, by the word of God, which liveth and abideth for ever   —*I Peter 1:23*

WHEN I MET HIM

I was young when I met the Master but I know
The skies that day were clear and more vividly blue
Than any I had seen. A heavenly glow
Trembled upon the hills and the world was new.

It also seemed to me the skylark's song
Was sweeter far than any I had heard
And a silent music swept my feet along
In an ecstasy too deep for any word.

I walked for a while on warmly hallowed ground
In a little country church with a star-white spire,
Where I met Jesus. And the joy I found
Was a flame that swept my heart with a holy fire!
          —*Sybil Leonard Armes*

THE NEW BIRTH

'Tis a new life;—thoughts move not as they did
With slow uncertain steps across my mind,
In thronging haste fast pressing on they bid
The portals open to the viewless wind
That comes not save when in the dust is laid
The crown of pride that gilds each mortal brow,
And from before man's vision melting fade
The heavens and earth;—their walls are falling now.—
Fast crowding on, each thought asks utterance strong;
Storm-lifted waves swift rushing to the shore;
On from the sea they send their shouts along,
Back through the cave-worn rocks their thunders roar;
And I a child of God by Christ made free
Start from death's slumbers to Eternity.
          —*Jones Very*

THE NINETY AND NINE

There were ninety and nine that safely lay
In the shelter of the fold,
   But one was out on the hills away,
   Far off from the gates of gold—
Away on the mountains wild and bare,
Away from the tender Shepherd's care.

"Lord, Thou hast here Thy ninety and nine;
Are they not enough for Thee?"
   But the Shepherd made answer: "This of mine
   Has wandered away from me,
And although the road be rough and steep,
I go to the desert to find my sheep."

But none of the ransomed ever knew
How deep were the waters crossed;
   Nor how dark was the night that the Lord passed through
   Ere He found His sheep that was lost.
Out in the desert He heard its cry—
Sick and helpless, and ready to die.

"Lord, whence are those blooddrops all the way
That mark out the mountain's track?"
   "They were shed for one who had gone astray
   Ere the Shepherd could bring him back."
"Lord, whence are Thy hands so rent and torn?"
"They're pierced tonight by many a thorn."

But all through the mountains, thunder-riven,
And up from the rocky steep,
   There arose a glad cry to the gate of heaven,
   "Rejoice! I have found my sheep!"
And the angels echoed around the throne,
"Rejoice, for the Lord brings back His own!"
                   —*Elizabeth C. Clephane*

Just as Thou Art

Just as thou art—without one trace
Of love, or joy, or inward grace,
Or meetness for the heavenly place,
    O guilty sinner! come.

Thy sins I bore on Calvary's tree,
The stripes, thy due, were laid on Me,
That peace and pardon might be free—
    O wretched sinner! come.

Come, leave thy burden at the cross;
Count all thy gains but empty dross;
My grace repays all earthly loss—
    O needy sinner! come.

Come, hither bring thy boding fears,
Thy aching heart, thy bursting tears;
'Tis mercy's voice salutes thine ears;
    O trembling sinner! come.

"The Spirit and the bride say, Come!"
Rejoicing saints re-echo, "Come!"
Who faints, who thirsts, who will, may come—
    Thy Saviour bids thee come!

PEACE

But the fruit of the Spirit is love, joy, peace— Galatians 5:22

Lift Up Your Hearts

Lift up your hearts. Life's inner spring
    A sudden flow of peace may bring;
    Trust all to God; 'tis there we find

A world perplexing left behind.
The heart upraised its Lord to meet
Drops every burden at His feet.
—*Mrs. D. R. H. Goodale*

THY PEACE

"He giveth quietness." O Elder Brother,
Whose homeless feet have pressed our path of pain,
Whose hands have borne the burden of our sorrow,
That in Thy losses we might find our gain,

Of all Thy gifts and infinite consolings
I ask but this: In every troubled hour
To hear Thy voice through all the tumult stealing,
And rest serene beneath its tranquil power.

Cares cannot fret me if my soul be dwelling
In the still air of faith's untroubled day;
Grief cannot shake me if I walk beside Thee,
My hand in Thine along the darkening way.

Content to know there comes a radiant morning
When from all shadows I shall find release:
Serene to wait the rapture of its dawning,
Who can make trouble when Thou sendest peace?
—*Emily Huntington Miller*

FIERCE WAS THE WILD BILLOW

Fierce was the wild billow,
Dark was the night,
Oars laboured heavily,
Foam glimmered white;
Mariners trembled,
Peril was nigh,—
Then said the God of God:
"Peace! it is I."

Ridge of the mountain-wave,
    Lower thy crest!
Wail of the stormy wind,
    Be thou at rest!
Peril can none be,
    Sorrow must fly,
When, saith the Light of Light:
    "Peace! it is I."

Jesu! Deliverer!
    Come Thou to me!
Soothe Thou my voyaging
    Over life's sea!
Thou, when the storm of death
    Roars, sweeping by,
Whisper, O Truth of Truth!
    "Peace! it is I."

                    —*Anatolius*

In Acceptance Lieth Peace

He said, "I will forget the dying faces;
The empty places,
They shall be filled again.
O voices moaning deep within me, cease."
But vain the word; vain, vain:
Not in forgetting lieth peace.

He said, "I will crowd action upon action,
The strife of faction
Shall stir me and sustain;
O tears that drown the fire of manhood cease."
But vain the word; vain, vain:
Not in endeavour lieth peace.

He said, "I will withdraw me and be quiet,
Why meddle in life's riot?
Shut be my door to pain.

Desire, thou dost befool me, thou shalt cease."
But vain the word; vain, vain:
Not in aloofness lieth peace.

He said, "I will submit; I am defeated.
God hath depleted
My life of its rich gain.
O futile murmurings, why will ye not cease?"
But vain the word; vain, vain:
Not in submission lieth peace.

He said, "I will accept the breaking sorrow
Which God to-morrow
Will to His son explain."
Then did the turmoil deep within him cease.
Not vain the word, not vain;
For in Acceptance lieth peace.
                              —*Amy Carmichael*

QUIETNESS

"Be still and know that I am God,"
That I who made and gave thee life
Will lead thy faltering steps aright;
That I who see each sparrow's fall
Will hear and heed thy earnest call.
        I am God.

"Be still and know that I am God,"
When aching burdens crush thy heart,
Then know I form thee for thy part
And purpose in the plan I hold.
        Trust in God.

"Be still and know that I am God,"
Who made the atom's tiny span
And set it moving to My plan,
That I who guide the stars above

Will guide and keep thee in My love.
Be thou still.

—*Doran*

In Thy Love

My spirit longs for thee
    Within my troubled breast,
Though I unworthy be
    Of so divine a Guest.

Of so divine a Guest
    Unworthy though I be,
Yet has my heart no rest
    Unless it come from thee.

Unless it come from thee,
    In vain I look around;
In all that I can see
    No rest is to be found.

No rest is to be found
    But in thy blessed love:
O, let my wish be crowned,
    And send it from above!

—*John Byrom*

The Place of Peace

At the heart of the cyclone tearing the sky
And flinging the clouds and the towers by,
    Is a place of central calm:
So here in the roar of mortal things,
I have a place where my spirit sings,
    In the hollow of God's Palm.

—*Edwin Markham*

GOD ALONE SUFFICES

Let nothing disturb thee;
Let nothing dismay thee;
All things pass:
God never changes.
Patience attains
All that it strives for.
He who has God
Finds he lacks nothing:
God alone suffices.

—*St. Teresa*

PEACE, PERFECT PEACE

Peace, perfect peace, in this dark world of sin?
The blood of Jesus whispers peace within.

Peace, perfect peace, by thronging duties pressed?
To do the will of Jesus, this is rest.

Peace, perfect peace, with sorrows surging round?
On Jesus' bosom naught but calm is found.

Peace, perfect peace, with loved ones far away?
In Jesus' keeping we are safe, and they.

Peace, perfect peace, our future all unknown?
Jesus we know, and he is on the throne.

Peace, perfect peace, death shadowing us and ours?
Jesus has vanquished death and all its powers.

It is enough: earth's struggles soon shall cease,
And Jesus call us to heaven's perfect peace.

—*E. H. Bickersteth*

"HE SHALL SPEAK PEACE UNTO THE NATIONS"
(*Zechariah 9:10*)

A stormy sea! Waves dashing high!
   The frail boat rocks upon the deep.
(How can the Lord unconscious lie,
   Head pillowed, in the stern—asleep?)

The winds sweep down on Galilee,
   And fiercer grows the storm, until
Strong men cry out in fear! Then He,
   In conscious power, speaks: "Peace, be still."

A world war-wrecked! In fury tossed
   By storms of rage and jealous hate!
(The Lord unmindful of the cost;
   Unheeding—till it be too late!)

Yet say not so! He hears the cry—
   And still "He maketh wars to cease."
The crucible is 'neath His eye.
   In His own time "He shall speak peace."
         —*Lila V. Walters*

PRAYER

. . . golden vials full of odours, which are the prayers of saints
         —*Revelation 5:8*

THOU ART COMING TO A KING

Thou art coming to a King,
Large petitions with thee bring
For His grace and power are such
None can ever ask too much.
         —*John Newton*

ALTARS

Let every corner of this day
Become an altar, Lord, for Thee,
A quiet place where I can pray
And hear Thee talk to me.

The bright expectancy of dawn
Will not endure the noonday heat,
Unless refreshing strength is drawn
Where altars touch Thy feet.
—*Sybil Leonard Armes*

PROOF

If radio's slim fingers
Can pluck a melody
From night, and toss it over
A continent or sea;

If the petaled white notes
Of a violin
Are blown across a mountain,
Or a city's din;

If songs, like crimson roses,
Are culled from thin blue air,
Why should mortals wonder
If God hears prayer?
—*Ethel Romig Fuller*
(from *Kitchen Sonnets*)

WHAT MORE CAN YOU ASK

God's love endureth forever—
What a wonderful thing to know
When the tides of life run against you
And your spirit is downcast and low . . .

God's kindness is ever around you,
Always ready to freely impart
Strength to your faltering spirit,
Cheer to your lonely heart . . .
God's presence is ever beside you,
As near as the reach of your hand,
You have but to tell Him your troubles,
There is nothing He won't understand . . .
And knowing God's love is unfailing,
And His mercy unending and great,
You have but to trust in His promise—
"God comes not too soon or too late" . . .
So wait with a heart that is patient
For the goodness of God to prevail—
For never do prayers go unanswered,
And His mercy and love never fail.

              —*Helen Steiner Rice*

PREVAILING PRAYER

Lord, what a change within us one short hour
Spent in Thy presence would prevail to make!
What heavy burdens from our bosoms take,
What parched grounds revive as with a shower;
We kneel, and all around us seems to lower;
We rise, and all, the distant and the near
Stands forth a sunny outline brave and clear.
We kneel, how weak! we arise, how full of power!
Why, therefore, should we do ourselves this wrong,
Or others, that we are not always strong;
That we are ever overborne with care;
That we should ever weak or heartless be,
Anxious or troubled, when with us is prayer,
And joy and strength and courage are with Thee?

              —*Richard C. Trench*

LET US PRAY

We cannot tell how often as we pray
For some hurt one bewildered and distressed
The answer comes, but many times those hearts
Find sudden peace and rest.
Someone had prayed, and faith, a reaching hand
Took hold of God and brought Him down that day—
So many, many hearts have need of prayer—
Oh, let us pray.

THE SECRET

I met God in the morning
    When my day was at its best,
And His presence came like sunrise,
    Like a glory in my breast.

All day long the Presence lingered,
    All day long He stayed with me,
And we sailed in perfect calmness
    O'er a very troubled sea.

Other ships were blown and battered,
    Other ships were sore distressed,
But the winds that seemed to drive them
    Brought to us a peace and rest.

Then I thought of other mornings,
    With a keen remorse of mind,
When I too had loosed the moorings,
    With the Presence left behind.

So I think I know the secret,
    Learned from many a troubled way:
You must seek Him in the morning
    If you want Him through the day!
          —Ralph Spaulding Cushman

GOD ANSWERS PRAYER

I know not by what methods rare,
But this I know, God answers prayer.
I know that He has given His Word,
Which tells me prayer is always heard,
And will be answered, soon or late;
And so I pray, and calmly wait.

I know not if the blessing sought,
Will come in just the way I thought,
But leave my prayers with Him alone,
Whose will is wiser than my own,
Assured that He will grant my quest,
Or send some answer far more blest.

THE UNSEEN BRIDGE

There is a bridge, whereof the span
Is rooted in the heart of man,
And reaches, without pile or rod,
Unto the Great White Throne of God.
Its traffic is in human sighs
Fervently wafted to the skies;
'Tis the one pathway from despair;
And it is called the Bridge of Prayer.

—*Gilbert Thomas*

NOT WEIGHING . . . BUT PARDONING

There is a path which no fowl knoweth,
    Nor vulture's eye hath seen;
A path beside a viewless river
    Whose banks are always green,
For it is the way of prayer,
Holy Spirit, lead us there.

O lead us on, weigh not our merits,
   For we have none to weigh,
But Saviour, pardon our offences,
   Lead even us to-day,
Further in the way of prayer,
Holy Spirit, lead us there.

                    —Amy Carmichael

PRAYER

Prayer, the Church's banquet, Angels' age,
   God's breath in man returning to his birth,
The soul in paraphrase, heart in pilgrimage,
   The Christian plummet sounding heav'n and earth;

Engine against th' Almighty, sinner's tower,
   Reversèd thunder, Christ-side-piercing spear,
The six-days-world transposing in an hour,

Softness, and peace, and joy, and love, and bliss,
   Exalted Manna, gladness of the best,
   Heaven in ordinary, man well dressed,
The milky way, the bird of Paradise,

   Church-bells beyond the stars heard, the soul's blood,
   The land of spices, something understood.

                    —George Herbert

THE KNEELING CAMEL

The camel, at the close of day
   Kneels down upon the sandy plain
To have his burden lifted off
     And rest to gain.

My soul, thou too shouldst to thy knees
   When daylight draweth to a close.
And let thy Master lift thy load
     And grant repose:

Else how canst thou tomorrow meet,
   With all tomorrow's work to do,
If thou thy burden all the night
     Dost carry through?

The camel kneels at break of day
   To have his guide replace his load,
Then rises up again to take
     The desert road.

So thou shouldst kneel at morning's dawn
   That God may give thee daily care,
Assured that He no load too great
     Will make thee bear.
             —Anna Temple

WHAT IS PRAYER?

Prayer is the soul's sincere desire,
   Utter'd or unexpress'd;
The motion of a hidden fire
   That trembles in the breast.

Prayer is the burthen of a sigh,
   The falling of a tear,
The upward glancing of the eye,
   When none but God is near.

Prayer is the simplest form of speech
   That infant lips can try;
Prayer the sublimest strains that reach
   The Majesty on high.

Prayer is the contrite sinner's voice
   Returning from his ways,
While angels in their songs rejoice,
   And cry, Behold, he prays!

Prayer is the Christian's vital breath,
   The Christian's native air;

His watchword at the gates of death;
    He enters heaven with prayer.

The saints in prayer appear as one
    In word, and deed, and mind;
While with the Father and the Son
    Sweet fellowship they find.

Nor prayer is made by man alone:
    The Holy Spirit pleads;
And Jesus, on the eternal Throne,
    For mourners intercedes.

O Thou, by whom we come to God!
    The Life, the Truth, the Way!
The path of prayer Thyself hast trod:
    Lord! teach us how to pray!
              —James Montgomery

WHAT HAPPENED

Do you know what happened on that day
When, burdened for souls, you tried to pray?
Did you think you failed to touch the Throne
When your lips were dumb, your prayer a groan?

Over the sea in a hot, dry land,
A sower sowed with faltering hand—
But, lo! in that hour refreshing came:
God's servant spoke with a tongue of flame!
And souls long steeped in a land of night
Passed from gloom to marvelous light;
Away from idols they turned to God,
Finding their peace in Jesus' blood.
'Twas your faith had moved God's mighty hand,
His blessings poured down in a desert land.
              —Margaret D. Armstrong

THE MEANING OF PRAYER

A breath of prayer in the morning
  Means a day of blessing sure;
A breath of prayer in the evening
  Means a night of rest secure;

A breath of prayer in our weakness
  Means a clasp of a mighty hand;
A breath of prayer when we're lonely
  Means Someone to understand;

A breath of prayer in our sorrows
  Means comfort and peace and rest;
A breath of prayer in our doubtings
  Assures us the Lord knows best;

A breath of prayer in rejoicing
  Gives joy and added delight,
For they that remember God's goodness
  Go singing far into the night.

There's never a year nor a season
  That prayer may not bless every hour,
And never a soul need be helpless
  When linked with God's infinite power.
               —Frances McKinnon Morton

THE SECRET PLACE

There is a place where thou canst touch the eyes
  Of blinded men to instant, perfect sight;
There is a place where thou canst say, 'Arise!'
  To dying captives, bound in chains of night;
There is a place where thou canst reach the store
  Of hoarded gold and free it for the Lord;
There is a place—upon some distant shore—
  Where thou canst send the worker or the Word.

There is a place where Heaven's resistless power
   Responsive moves to thine insistent plea;
There is a place—a silent, trusting hour—
   Where God Himself descends and fights for thee.
Where is that blessed place—dost thou ask 'Where?'
   O soul, it is the secret place of prayer.
               —*Adelaide A. Pollard*

A PRAYER

Lord, make me an instrument of Thy peace.
Where there is hatred, let me sow love;
When there is injury, pardon;
Where there is doubt, faith;
When there is despair, hope;
Where there is darkness, light;
When there is sadness, joy.

O Divine Master, grant that
I may not so much seek
To be consoled, as to console;
Not so much to be understood as
To understand; not so much to be
Loved as to love:
For it is in giving that we receive;
It is in pardoning that we are pardoned;
It is in dying that we awaken to eternal life.
               —*Francis of Assisi*

RESURRECTION

*I am the resurrection, and the life: he that believeth
in me, though he were dead, yet shall he live*
                                        —John 11:25

EASTER

Most glorious Lord of life, that on this day,
    didst make thy triumph over death and sin:
    and having harrowed hell, didst bring away
    captivity thence captive us to win:
This joyous day, dear Lord, with joy begin,
    and grant that we for whom thou diddest die
    being with thy dear blood clean washed from sin,
    may live for ever in felicity.
And that thy love we weighing worthily,
    may likewise love thee for the same again:
    and for thy sake that all like dear didst buy,
    with love may one another entertain.
So let us love, dear love, like as we ought,
    love is the lesson which the Lord us taught.
                                        —Edmund Spenser

HE IS RISEN

He is risen! Earth awakes
And her prison house forsakes.
Hear the glad bird-voices sing—
"Where, O Death, is now thy sting?"
Winds their silver trumpets blow—
"He hath conquered every foe."
Soft the murmuring waters say—
"Lo, the stone is rolled away."
    He is risen, He is risen,
Christ the Lord is risen to-day.

He is risen! Heart, rejoice,
Hear you not the angel's voice?
Though you wait beside the tomb,
There is light within its gloom:
Grave, where is thy victory?
He hath set thy captives free,
He hath robbed thee of thy prey,
They with Him shall live alway.
    He is risen, He is risen,
Christ the Lord is risen to-day.
             —Annie Johnson Flint

A BETTER RESURRECTION

I have no wit, no words, no tears;
    My heart within me like a stone
Is numbed too much for hopes or fears;
    Look right, look left, I dwell alone;
I lift mine eyes, but dimmed with grief
    No everlasting hills I see;
My life is in the falling leaf:
    O Jesus, quicken me.

My life is like a faded leaf,
    My harvest dwindled to a husk;
Truly my life is void and brief
    And tedious in the barren dusk;
My life is like a frozen thing,
    No bud nor greenness can I see:
Yet rise it shall—the sap of Spring;
    O Jesus, rise in me.

My life is like a broken bowl,
    A broken bowl that cannot hold
One drop of water for my soul
    Or cordial in the searching cold;
Cast in the fire the perished thing,
    Melt and remould it, till it be
A royal cup for Him my King.
    O Jesus, drink of me.

—*Christina Rossetti*

THE VICTOR

The head that once was crowned with thorns
    Is crowned with glory now;
A royal diadem adorns
    The mighty victor's brow.

The highest place that heaven affords
    Is his, is his by right,
The King of kings, and Lord of lords,
    And heaven's eternal Light;

The joy of all who dwell above,
    The joy of all below,
To whom he manifests his love
    And grants his Name to know.

To them the cross with all its shame,
    With all its grace is given;
Their name, an everlasting name;
    Their joy, the joy of heaven.

They suffer with their Lord below,
    They reign with him above,
Their profit and their joy to know
    The mystery of his love.

The cross he bore is life and health,
    Though shame and death to him:

His people's hope, his people's wealth,
     Their everlasting theme.
                              —*Thomas Kelly*

SPRING SONG

"The earth is the Lord's and the fulness thereof"—
It speaks of His greatness and it sings of His love,
And the wonder and glory of the first Easter morn,
Like the first Christmas night when the Saviour was born,
Are blended together in symphonic splendor
And God with a voice that is gentle and tender
Speaks to all hearts attuned to His voice,
Bidding His listeners to gladly rejoice . . .
For He who was born to be crucified
Arose from the grave to be glorified . . .
And the birds in the trees and the flowers of Spring
All join in proclaiming this heavenly King.
                              —*Helen Steiner Rice*

JESUS LIVES

Jesus lives! thy terrors now
     Can no longer, death, appall us;
Jesus lives! by this we know
     Thou, O grave, canst not enthrall us.   Alleluia!

Jesus lives! henceforth is death
     But the gate of life immortal;
This shall calm our trembling breath,
     When we pass its gloomy portal.   Alleluia!

Jesus lives! for us he died;
     Then, alone to Jesus living,
Pure in heart may we abide,
     Glory to our Saviour giving.   Alleluia!

Jesus lives! our hearts know well
   Naught from us his love shall sever;
Life, nor death, nor powers of hell
   Tear us from his keeping ever.   Alleluia!

Jesus lives! to him the throne
   Over all the world is given:
May we go where he has gone,
   Rest and reign with him in heaven.   Alleluia!
                     —C. F. Gellert

SALVATION

*Therefore with joy shall ye draw water out of
the wells of salvation*   —Isaiah 12:3

POSSESSION

Heaven above is softer blue
   Earth beneath is sweeter green.
Something lives in every hue
   Christless eyes have never seen.
Birds with gladder songs o'erflow,
   Flowers with deeper beauty shine
Since I know as now I know
   I am His and He is mine.

I SOUGHT THE LORD

I sought the Lord, and afterward I knew
   He moved my soul to seek him, seeking me;
It was not I that found, O Saviour true;
   No, I was found of thee.

Thou didst reach forth thy hand and mine enfold;
   I walked and sank not on the storm-vexed sea;

'Twas not so much that I on thee took hold,
  As thou, dear Lord, on me.

I find, I walk, I love, but O the whole
  Of love is but my answer, Lord, to thee;
For thou wert long beforehand with my soul,
  Always thou lovedst me.

WITHIN THY HEART

I asked for Peace—
  My sins arose,
  And bound me close,
I could not find release.

I asked for Truth—
  My doubts came in,
  And with their din
They wearied all my youth.

I asked for Love—
  My lovers failed,
  And griefs assailed
Around, beneath, above.

I asked for Thee—
  And thou didst come
  To take me home
Within Thy Heart to be.
      —*Digby M. Dolben*

THE TOUCH OF THE MASTER'S HAND

'Twas battered and scarred, and the auctioneer
Thought it scarcely worth his while
To waste much time on the old violin,
But held it up with a smile.
"What am I bidden, good folks," he cried,
"Who will start bidding for me?

A dollar, a dollar"—then, "Two!" "Only two?
Two dollars, and who'll make it three?
Three dollars once; three dollars, twice;
Going for three—" But no,
From the room, far back, a gray-haired man
Came forward and picked up the bow;
Then, wiping the dust from the old violin,
And tightening the loose strings,
He played a melody pure and sweet
As sweet as a caroling angel sings.

The music ceased, and the auctioneer,
With a voice that was quiet and low,
Said, "What am I bidden for the old violin?"
And he held it up with the bow.
"A thousand dollars, and who'll make it two?
Two thousand! And who'll make it three?
Three thousand, once; three thousand, twice;
And going, and gone!" said he.
The people cheered, but some of them cried,
"We do not quite understand
What changed its worth?" Swift came the reply:
"The touch of the master's hand."

And many a man with life out of tune,
And battered and scattered with sin,
Is auctioned cheap to the thoughtless crowd,
Much like the old violin.
A "mess of pottage," a glass of wine;
A game—and he travels on.
He's "going" once, and "going" twice,
He's "going" and "almost gone."
But the Master comes, and the foolish crowd
Never can quite understand
The worth of a soul, and the change that's wrought
By the touch of the Master's hand.

—*Myra Brooks Welch*

FOR GOD SO LOVED

For God, the Lord of earth and Heaven,
So loved, and longed to see forgiven,
The world, in sin and pleasure mad,
That He gave the greatest gift He had—
His only son—to take our place,
That whosoever—Oh, what grace!—
Believeth, placing simple trust
In Him, the righteous and the just,
Should not perish, lost in sin,
But have eternal life in Him.
                    —*Barbara C. Ryberg*

THE PATH

So many hearts are like old battlefields
Where conflicts have been waged on every slope,
The bitter scars are there, the broken shields,
The fallow plains that once were green with hope.

But if forgiveness, like the gentle rain,
Can cleanse our hearts and melt the livid scars,
We shall ascend God's golden hills again,
In peace as white as His eternal stars!
                    —*Sybil Leonard Armes*

From THE HOUND OF HEAVEN

Now of that long pursuit
   Comes on at hand the bruit;
That Voice is round me like a bursting sea:
"And is thy earth so marred,
Shattered in shard on shard?
Lo, all things fly thee, for thou fliest Me!
      Strange, piteous, futile thing!
Wherefore should any set thee love apart?

Seeing none but I makes much of naught" (He said),
"And human love needs human meriting:
    How hast thou merited—
Of all man's clotted clay the dingiest clot?
    Alack, thou knowest not
How little worthy of any love thou art!
Whom wilt thou find to love ignoble thee,
    Save Me, save only Me?
All which I took from thee I did but take,
    Nor for thy harms,
But just that thou might'st seek it in My arms.
    All which thy child's mistake
Fancies as lost, I have stored for thee at home:
    Rise, clasp My hand, and come!"

    Halts by me that footfall:
    Is my gloom, after all,
Shade of His hand, outstretched caressingly?
    "Ah, fondest, blindest, weakest,
    I am He Whom thou seekest!
Thou dravest love from thee, who dravest Me."

                        —*Francis Thompson*

Hymn

    When storms arise
    And dark'ning skies
        About me threat'ning lower,
    To thee, O Lord, I raise mine eyes,
    To thee my tortured spirit flies
        For solace in that hour.

    Thy mighty arm
    Will let no harm
        Come near me nor befall me;
    Thy voice shall quiet my alarm,
    When life's great battle waxeth warm—
    No foeman shall appall me.

Upon thy breast
Secure I rest,
    From sorrow and vexation;
No more my sinful cares oppressed,
But in thy presence ever blest,
    O God of my salvation.
                    —*Paul Laurence Dunbar*

Take Him

Nay, do not wrong Him by thy heavy thoughts,
    But love His love.
Do thou full justice to His tenderness,
    His mercy prove;
Take Him for what He is, O take Him all,
    And look above!
                    —*Horatius Bonar.*

SECOND COMING

*Behold, he cometh with clouds; and every
eye shall see him   —Revelation 1:7*

From Saint Paul

Hark what a sound, and too divine for hearing,
    Stirs on the earth and trembles in the air!
Is it the thunder of the Lord's appearing?
    Is it the music of His people's prayer?

Surely He cometh, and a thousand voices
    Shout to the saints and to the deaf are dumb;
Surely He cometh, and the earth rejoices
    Glad in His coming Who hath sworn, I come.
                    —*Frederic W. H. Myers*

The Footfall

Do we not hear Thy footfall, O Belovèd,
   Among the stars on many a moonless night?
Do we not catch the whisper of Thy coming
   On winds of dawn, and often in the light
Of noontide and of sunset almost see Thee?
   Look up through shining air
And long to see Thee, O Belovèd, long to see Thee,
   And wonder that Thou art not standing there?

And we shall hear Thy footfall, O Belovèd,
   And starry ways will open, and the night
Will call her candles from their distant stations,
   And winds shall sing Thee, noon, and mingled light
Of rose-red evening thrill with lovely welcome;
   And we, caught up in air,
Shall see Thee, O Belovèd, we shall see Thee,
   In hush of adoration see Thee there.

                    —*Amy Carmichael*

Come, Lord Jesus

Because of little children soiled,
And disinherited, despoiled,

Because of hurt things, feathered, furred,
Tormented beast, imprisoned bird,

Because of many-folded grief,
Beyond redress, beyond belief,

Because the word is true that saith,
The whole creation travaileth—

Of all our prayers this is the sum:
O come, Lord Jesus, come.

                    —*Amy Carmichael*

QUITE SUDDENLY

Quite suddenly—it may at the turning of a lane,
Where I stand to watch a skylark soar from out the swelling grain,
That the trump of God shall thrill me, with its call so loud and clear,
And I'm called away to meet Him, whom of all I hold most dear.

Quite suddenly—it may be in His house I bend my knee,
When the Kingly voice, long-hoped-for, comes at last to summon
    me,
And the fellowship of earth-life that has seemed so passing sweet,
Proves nothing but the shadow of our meeting round His feet.

Quite suddenly—it may be as I tread the busy street,
Strong to endure life's stress and strain, its every call to meet,
That through the roar of traffic, a trumpet, silvery clear,
Shall stir my startled senses and proclaim His coming near.

Quite suddenly—it may be as I lie in dreamless sleep,
God's gift to many a sorrowing heart, with no more tears to weep,
That a call shall break my slumber and a Voice sound in my ear;
"Rise up, My love, and come away! Behold, the Bridegroom's
    here!"

SOON THOU WILT COME

Soon Thou wilt come—oh, blest anticipation!—
    And we shall gaze unhindered on Thy face;
Our longing hope shall have its glad fruition,
    And in those wounds we shall love's story trace.

Oh, cloudless morn of heavenly light and gladness,
    When God Himself shall wipe all tears away!
There shall be no more death and no more sadness,
    No trace of sin through God's eternal day.
                                        —*J. W. H. Nichols*

BE YE ALSO READY

"What are the signs of Thy coming,
    And when shall the end-time be?"
Anxious, they questioned the Master,
    Curious, even as we.

Are these the signs of His coming
    That loom over sea and land,
That darken the earth and the heavens?
    Is the day so near at hand?

We know not; He hath not told us
    This secret of the Lord,
But all we need He hath left us
    To read in His sacred word.

And pulsing through the silence
    Like the far, faint throb of a drum;
"Watch, be ye also ready,
    For ye know not when I come."

Sweet as a silver trumpet
    Through tumult and clamor clear;
"Watch, be ye also ready,
    For the time is drawing near."
            —*Annie Johnson Flint*

THE DAY

The day of reappearing! how it speeds!
    He who is true and faithful speaks the word.
Then shall we ever be with those we love—
    Then shall we be forever with the Lord.

Short death and darkness! Endless life and light!
    Short dimming; endless shining in yon sphere,
Where all is incorruptible and pure;—
    The joy without the pain, the smile without the tear.
            —*Horatius Bonar*

IF HE SHOULD COME TODAY

If He should come today
  And find I had not told
  One soul about my Heavenly Friend
  Whose blessings all my way attend,
What would He say?

If He should come today
  Would I be glad—quite glad?
  Remembering He had died for all
  And none, through me, had heard His call,
What would I say?

          —*Grace E. Troy*

HE IS COMING

He is coming, O my spirit! with His everlasting peace,
  With His blessedness immortal and complete.
He is coming, O my spirit! and His coming brings release.
  I listen for the coming of His feet.

STEWARDSHIP

Keep that which is committed to thy trust   *—I Timothy 6:20*

HARVEST

Sow love, and taste its fruitage pure;
  Sow peace, and reap its harvest bright;
Sow sunbeams on the rock and moor,
  And reap a harvest-home of light.
          —*Horatius Bonar*

STEWARD OF GOD

Help me to spend
Carefully, prayerfully,
Substance Thou lendest me.
Help me to tend,
Prayerfully, carefully,
Tasks which Thou sendest me.

Help me to use,
Carefully, prayerfully.
Talents Thou gavest me.
Help me to choose
Prayerfully, carefully,
O Christ that savest me!
—*Martha Snell Nicholson*

SERVICE

Across the boughs of a swinging, sunlit tree
A scarlet robin's buoyant, lilting song
Pours from his little throat deliriously,
And makes my heart to sing the whole day long.

Out in my garden lifts the crimson heart
Of a rose, full blown, drenched by the dews of dawn,
Its velvet petals will soon fall apart
But in my heart its fragrance will live on.

Perhaps it's true in every ministry
That he serves best who serves unconsciously.
—*Sybil Leonard Armes*

AS A MAN SOWETH

We must not hope to be mowers,
    And to gather the ripe gold ears,

Unless we have first been sowers
   And watered the furrows with tears.

It is not just as we take it,
   This mystical world of ours,
Life's field will yield as we make it
   A harvest of thorns or of flowers.
      —Johann Wolfgang Von Goethe

IS THERE SOME DESERT

Is there some desert or some pathless sea
Where thou, good God of angels, wilt send me?
Some oak for me to rend; some sod,
Some rock for me to break;
Some handful of his corn to take
And scatter far afield,
Till it, in turn, shall yield
Its hundred fold
Of grains of gold
To feed the waiting children of my God.
Show me the desert, Father, or the sea.
Is it thine enterprise? Great God, send me.
      —Edward Everett Hale

WHO LIVETH WELL

He liveth long who liveth well;
   All else is being flung away;
He liveth longest who can tell
   Of true things truly done each day.

Fill up each hour with what will last;
   Use well the moments as they go;
The life above, when this is past,
   Is the ripe fruit of life below.
      —Horatius Bonar

We Give Thee but Thine Own

We give thee but thine own,
Whate'er the gift may be;
All that we have is thine alone,
A trust, O Lord, from thee.

May we thy bounties thus
As stewards true receive,
And gladly, as thou blessest us,
To thee our first-fruits give.

—William Walsham How

In Thy Hand

Bless Thou the gifts our hands have brought,
  Bless Thou the work our hearts have planned;
Ours is the faith, the will, the thought,
  The rest, O God, is in Thy hand.

—Samuel Longfellow

A Bag of Tools

Isn't it strange
That princes and kings,
And clowns that caper
In sawdust rings,
And common people
Like you and me
Are builders for eternity?

Each is given a bag of tools,
A shapeless mass,
A book of rules;
And each must make,
Ere life is flown,
A stumbling-block
Or a stepping-stone.

—R. L. Sharpe

HIS STRENGTH

And, as the path of duty is made plain,
May grace be given that I may walk therein,
Not like the hireling, for his selfish gain,
With backward glances and reluctant tread,
Making a merit of his coward dread,—
But, cheerful, in the light around me thrown,
Walking as one to pleasant service led;
Doing God's will as if it were my own,
Yet trusting not in mine, but in His strength alone!
                    —*John Greenleaf Whittier*

GIVE

There are loyal hearts, there are spirits brave,
    There are souls that are pure and true;
Then give to the world the best you have,
    And the best will come back to you.
Give love, and love to your life will flow,
    A strength in your utmost need;
Have faith, and a score of hearts will show
    Their faith in your word and deed.
                    —*Madeline S. Bridges*

THANKSGIVING

It is a good thing to give thanks unto the Lord—Psalm 92:1

SUNSET

For the great red rose of sunset,
Dropping petals on the way
For the tired feet of day,
    Thanks to Thee, our Father.

For the violet of twilight
Singing, "Hush, ye children, hush,"
For the after-glow's fair flush,
   Thanks to Thee, our Father.

For the softly sliding darkness
Wherein many jewels are,
Kindly-eye'd, familiar,
   Thanks to Thee, our Father.

For the comfort of forgiveness
Taking from us our offence,
Steeping us in innocence,
   Thanks to Thee, our Father.

For the viewless, tall, white angels
Bidden to ward off from us
All things foul, calamitous,
   Thanks to Thee, our Father.

That Thy love sets not with sunset,
Nor with starset, nor with moon,
But is ever one high noon,
   Thanks to Thee, our Father.
                    —*Amy Carmichael*

GRATITUDE

O Thou, whose bounty fills my cup
   With every blessing meet!
I give Thee thanks for every drop—
   The bitter and the sweet.
I praise Thee for the desert road,
   And for the riverside;
For all Thy goodness hath bestowed,
   And all Thy grace denied.
                    —*Jane Crewdson*

NOW THANK WE ALL OUR GOD

Now thank we all our God,
With heart and hands and voices,
Who wondrous things hath done,
In whom his world rejoices;
Who from our mother's arms
Hath blessed us on our way
With countless gifts of love,
And still is ours to-day.

O may this bounteous God
Through all our life be near us,
With ever joyful hearts
And blessed peace to cheer us;
And keep us in his grace,
And guide us when perplexed,
And free us from all ills
In this world and the next.

All praise and thanks to God
The Father now be given,
The Son, and him who reigns
With them in highest heaven,
The One eternal God
Whom heaven and earth adore;
For thus it was, is now,
And shall be evermore.
                            —*Martin Rinkart*

TRIALS

*In the world ye shall have tribulation: but be of good
cheer; I have overcome the world   —John 16:33*

ALL'S WELL

The clouds, which rise with thunder, slake
    Our thirsty souls with rain;
The blow most dreaded falls to break
    From off our limbs a chain;
And wrongs of man to man but make
    The love of God more plain.
As through the shadowy lens of even
    The eye looks farthest into heaven
On gleams of star and depths of blue
    The glaring sunshine never knew!
            —*John Greenleaf Whittier*

WHAT GOD HATH PROMISED

God hath not promised
Skies always blue,
Flower-strewn pathways
All our lives through;
God hath not promised
Sun without rain,
Joy without sorrow,
Peace without pain.

But God hath promised
Strength for the day,
Rest for the labor,
Light for the way,
Grace for the trials,
Help from above,
Unfailing sympathy,
Undying love.
    —*Annie Johnson Flint*

ON A SICK BED

O my Lord, how Thy compassion
All the weary night,
Doth sustain me, never failing,
New each morning light!

Though the outward man shall perish,
Yet the inward man
Daily is renewed. I thank Thee
That Thy Spirit can

Conquer suffering flesh, and quicken
This poor fainting soul,
Till at last it sweeps, triumphant,
To its wondrous goal!
    —*Martha Snell Nicholson*

WAIT

Planted by the Master's hand,
Steadfast in thy place to stand
While the ever-changing year
Clothes or strips thy branches bare;
Lending not a leaf to hold

Warmth against the winter's cold,
Lightening not a limb the less
For the summer's sultriness;
Nay, thy burden heavier made,
That within thy bending shade
Thankless multitudes oppressed
There may lay them down and rest,—
Soul, upon thy Calvary
Wait; the Christ will come to thee.

—John Banister Tabb

HIS APPOINTMENT

Disappointment, *His appointment;*
    Change one letter, then I see
That the thwarting of my purpose
    Is God's better choice for me.
His appointment must be blessing,
    Though it may come in disguise,
For the end from the beginning
    Open to His wisdom lies.

—Edith L. Young

SHUT IN WITH GOD

Shut in with God! O wondrous thought:
Shut in with the peace His sufferings brought;
Shut in with the love that wields the rod:
O company blest! Shut in with God!

BLIND BUT HAPPY

O what a happy soul am I!
    Although I cannot see,

I am resolved that in this world
   Contented I will be;
How many blessings I enjoy
   That other people don't!
To weep and sigh because I'm blind,
   I cannot, and I won't.
             —*Fanny J. Crosby*

LET ME GROW

What though my lot is a lonely place
   And my spirit behind the bars?
All the day long I may look at the sun,
   And at night look out at the stars.
Dear God! let me grow from day to day
   Clinging and sunny and bright!
Though planted in shade, Thy window is near,
   And my leaves may turn to the light.
             —*Mary Mapes Dodge*

IN HOURS OF DISCOURAGEMENT
GOD IS OUR ENCOURAGEMENT

Sometimes we feel uncertain
And unsure of everything,
Afraid to make decisions,
Dreading what the day will bring—
We keep wishing it were possible
To dispel all fear and doubt
And to understand more readily
Just what life is all about—
God has given us the answers
Which too often go unheeded,
But if we search His promises
We'll find everything that's needed

To lift our faltering spirits
And renew our courage, too,
For there's absolutely nothing
Too much for God to do—
For the Lord is our salvation
And our strength in every fight,
Our redeemer and protector,
Our eternal guiding light—
He has promised to sustain us,
He's our refuge from all harms,
And underneath this refuge
Are the everlasting arms—
So cast your burden on Him,
Seek His counsel when distressed,
And go to Him for comfort
When you're lonely and oppressed—
For God is our encouragement
In trouble and in trials,
And in suffering and in sorrow
He will turn our tears to smiles.

—Helen Steiner Rice

PAIN

The dark brown mould's upturned
By the sharp-pointed plow;
And I've a lesson learned.

My life is but a field,
Stretched out beneath God's sky,
Some harvest rich to yield.

Where grows the golden grain?
Where faith? Where sympathy?
In a furrow cut by pain.

—Maltbie D. Babcock.

PRAYER ANSWERED BY CROSSES

I asked the Lord that I might grow
    In faith, and love, and every grace;
Might more of His salvation know,
    And seek more earnestly His face.

'Twas He who taught me thus to pray,
    And He, I trust, has answered prayer;
But it has been in such a way
    As almost drove me to despair.

I hoped that in some favoured hour
    At once He'd answer my request,
And by His love's constraining power,
    Subdue my sins and give me rest.

Instead of this, He made me feel
    The hidden evils of my heart,
And let the angry powers of hell
    Assault my soul in every part.

Yea, more—with His own hand He seemed
    Intent to aggravate my woe;
Crossed all the fair designs I schemed,
    Blasted my gourds, and laid me low.

"Lord, why is this?" I, trembling, cried;
    "Wilt Thou pursue Thy worm to death?"
" 'Tis in this way," the Lord replied,
    "I answer prayer for grace and faith.

"These inward trials I employ
    From self and pride to set thee free,
And break thy schemes of earthly joy,
    That thou may'st seek thy all in me."
                —*John Newton*

TRUST

Whoso trusteth in the Lord, happy is he—Proverbs 16:20

WHY?

Rain, rain
Beating against the pane!
How endlessly it pours
Out of doors
From the blackened sky—
I wonder why!

Flowers, flowers,
Upspringing after showers,
Blossoming fresh and fair,
Everywhere!
Ah, God has explained
Why it rained!

PROPS

Earthly props are useless,
On Thy grace I fall;
Earthly strength is weakness,
Father, on Thee I call,—
For comfort, strength, and guidance,
O, give me all!

—John Oxenham

TWO PRAYERS

Last night my little boy confessed to me
Some childish wrong;

And kneeling at my knee,
He prayed with tears—
"Dear God, make me a man
Like Daddy—wise and strong;
I know You can."

Then while he slept
I knelt beside his bed,
Confessed my sins,
And prayed with low-bowed head—
"O God, make me a child
Like my child here—
Pure, guileless,
Trusting Thee with faith sincere."
                              —*Andrew Gillies*

From THE MARSHES OF GLYNN

As the marsh-hen secretly builds on the watery sod,
Behold I will build me a nest on the greatness of God:
I will fly in the greatness of God as the marsh-hen flies
In the freedom that fills all the space 'twixt the marsh and the skies:
By so many roots as the marsh-grass sends in the sod
I will heartily lay me a-hold on the greatness of God:
Oh, like to the greatness of God is the greatness within
The range of the marshes, the liberal marshes of Glynn.
                              —*Sidney Lanier*

ARIDITY

O Soul, canst thou not understand
Thou art not left alone,
As a dog to howl and moan
His master's absence? Thou art as a book
Left in a room that He forsook,
But returns to by and by,

A book of His dear choice,—
That quiet waiteth for His Hand,
That quiet waiteth for His Eye,
That quiet waiteth for His Voice.

—Michael Field

COMPLAINTS

I think we are too ready with complaint
  In this fair world of God's. Had we no hope
  Indeed beyond the zenith and the slope
Of yon gray bank of sky, we might be faint
To muse upon eternity's constraint
  Round our aspirant souls. But since the scope
  Must widen early, is it well to droop
For a few days consumed in loss and taint?
O pusillanimous Heart, be comforted,—
  And, like a cheerful traveller, take the road
Singing beside the hedge. What if the bread
  Be bitter in thine inn, and thou unshod
To meet the flints?—At least it may be said,
  "Because the way is *short,* I thank Thee, God!"

—Elizabeth Barrett Browning

DON'T WORRY

Why shadow the beauty of sea or of land
  With a doubt or a fear?
God holds all the swift-rolling worlds in His hand,
And sees what no man can as yet understand,
  That out of life here,
  With its smile and its tear,
Comes forth into light, from eternity planned,
  The soul of good cheer.
  Don't worry—
  The end shall appear.

—Elizabeth Porter Gould

WHAT THE BIRDS DO

O wise little birds, how do you know
    The way to go,
Southward or northward, to and fro?

Far up in the ether pipèd they:
    "We but obey
One who calleth us far away.

"He calleth and calleth year by year,
    Now there, now here;
Ever He maketh the way appear."

Dear little birds! He calleth me
    Who calleth ye:
Would that I might as trusting be!
      —Harriet McEwen Kimball

HOLDING

In the bitter waves of woe,
    Beaten and tossed about
By the sullen winds that blow
    From the desolate shores of doubt,
Where the anchors that faith has cast
    Are dragging in the gale,
I am quietly holding fast
    To the things that cannot fail.
      —Washington Gladden

A MIGHTY FORTRESS

A mighty fortress is our God,
    A bulwark never failing;
Our helper he amid the flood
    Of mortal ills prevailing:
For still our ancient foe

Doth seek to work us woe;
His craft and power are great,
And, armed with cruel hate,
   On earth is not his equal.

Did we in our own strength confide,
   Our striving would be losing,
Were not the right man on our side,
   The man of God's own choosing:
Dost ask who that may be?
Christ Jesus, it is he;
Lord Sabaoth his Name,
From age to age the same,
   And he must win the battle.

And though this world, with devils filled,
   Should threaten to undo us,
We will not fear, for God hath willed
   His truth to triumph through us:
The prince of darkness grim,
We tremble not for him;
His rage we can endure,
For lo! his doom is sure,
   One little word shall fell him.

That word above all earthly powers,
   No thanks to them, abideth;
The Spirit and the gifts are ours
   Through him who with us sideth:
Let goods and kindred go,
This mortal life also;
The body they may kill:
God's truth abideth still,
   His kingdom is for ever.
                    —Martin Luther

HIS PURPOSES

The shuttles of His purpose move
    To carry out His own design;
Seek not too soon to disapprove
    His work, nor yet assign
Dark motives, when, with silent tread,
    You view some sombre fold;
For lo, within each darker thread
    There twines a thread of gold.

    Spin cheerfully,
    Not tearfully,
He knows the way you plod;
    Spin carefully,
    Spin prayerfully,
But leave the thread with God.

VICTORIOUS LIVING

*Now thanks be unto God, which always causeth us
to triumph in Christ   —II Corinthians 2:14*

PER ASPERA

Thank God, a man can grow!
He is not bound
With earthward gaze to creep along the ground:
Though his beginnings be but poor and low,
Thank God, a man can grow!
The fire upon his altars may burn dim,
    The torch he lighted may in darkness fail,
    And nothing to rekindle it avail,—

Yet high beyond his dull horizon's rim,
Arcturus and the Pleiades beckon him.
                    —*Florence Earle Coates*

JESUS, I AM RESTING, RESTING

Jesus, I am resting, resting
    In the joy of what Thou art,
I am finding out the greatness
    Of Thy loving heart.
Here I gaze and gaze upon Thee,
    As Thy beauty fills my soul,
For by Thy transforming power,
    Thou hast made me whole.

O how great Thy loving-kindness,
    Vaster, broader than the sea;
O how marvellous Thy goodness
    Lavished all on me—
Yes, I rest in Thee, Beloved,
    Know what wealth of grace is Thine,
Know Thy certainty of promise
    And have made it mine.

Simply trusting Thee, Lord Jesus,
    I behold Thee as Thou art,
And Thy love, so pure, so changeless,
    Satisfies my heart,
Satisfies its deepest longing,
    Meets, supplies my every need,
Compasseth me round with blessings:
    Thine is love indeed.

Ever lift Thy face upon me
   As I work and wait for Thee;
Resting 'neath Thy smile, Lord Jesus,
   Earth's dark shadows flee.
Brightness of my Father's glory,
   Sunshine of my Father's face,
Let Thy glory e'er shine on me,
   Fill me with Thy grace.

      —Jean Sophia Pigott

JESUS AND I

I cannot do it alone;
   The waves run fast and high,
And the fogs close chill around,
   And the light goes out in the sky;
But I know that we two shall win in the end—
   Jesus and I.

I cannot row it myself,
   My boat on the raging sea;
But beside me sits Another,
   Who pulls or steers with me;
And I know that we too shall come into port—
   His child and He.

Coward and wayward and weak,
   I change with the changing sky,
Today so eager and brave,
   Tomorrow not caring to try;
But He never gives in, so we two shall win—
   Jesus and I.

Strong and tender and true,
   Crucified once for me;
Never will He change, I know,
   Whatever I may be;

But all He says I must do,
　　Ever from sin to keep free.
We shall finish our course and reach home at last—
　　His child and He.

　　　　　　　　　　　　—Dan Crawford

SUNSHINE

Just a song of sunshine!
　　Let it flood the heart,
And of life's completeness
　　Let it form a part.
Sing it though it cost you
　　Hours of grief and pain,
You will reap a harvest
　　Deep of golden grain,
Oh, the joy and comfort
　　You through life may know,
With a song of sunshine
　　Everywhere you go!

LESS OF SELF

Less, less of self each day
　　And more, my God, of Thee;
Oh, keep me in Thy way,
　　However rough it be.

Less of the flesh each day,
　　Less of the world and sin;
More of Thy love, I pray,
　　More of Thyself within.

Riper and riper now,
　　Each hour let me become;
Less fond of things below,
　　More fit for such a home.

More moulded to Thy will,
    Lord, let Thy servant be;
Higher and higher still—
    Nearer and nearer Thee.

OBEDIENCE

I said, "Let me walk in the fields."
    He said, "No, walk in the town."
I said, "There are no flowers there."
    He said, "No flowers, but a crown."

I said, "But the skies are black;
    There is nothing but noise and din."
And He wept as he sent me back;
    "There is more," He said; "there is sin."

I said, "But the air is thick,
    And fogs are veiling the sun."
He answered, "Yet souls are sick,
    And souls in the dark undone."

I said, "I shall miss the light,
    And friends will miss me, they say."
He answered, "Choose to-night
    If *I* am to miss you, or they."

I pleaded for time to be given.
    He said, "Is it hard to decide?
It will not seem hard in heaven
    To have followed the steps of your Guide."

I cast one look at the fields,
    Then set my face to the town;
He said, "My child, do you yield?
    Will you leave the flowers for the crown?"

Then into His hand went mine,
    And into my heart came He;

And I walk in a light divine
  The path I had feared to see.
                     —*George Macdonald*

NONE OF SELF AND ALL OF THEE

Oh, the bitter shame and sorrow
  That a time could ever be
When I let the Saviour's pity
Plead in vain, and proudly answered,
  "All of self and none of Thee."

Yet He found me; I beheld Him
  Bleeding on the accursed tree;
Heard Him pray, "Forgive them, Father";
And my wistful heart said faintly,
  "Some of self and some of Thee."

Day by day, His tender mercy,
  Healing, helping, full and free,
Sweet and strong, and, oh, so patient,
Brought me lower, while I whispered,
  "Less of self and more of Thee."

Higher than the highest heavens,
  Deeper than the deepest sea,
Lord, *Thy love* at last has conquered;
Grant me now my soul's desire,
  "None of self and all of Thee."
                     —*Theodore Monod*

GET SOMEWHERE

Are you groping for a blessing,
  Never getting there?
Listen to a word in season,
  Get somewhere.

Are you struggling for salvation
   By your anxious prayer?
Stop your struggling, simply trust, and—
   Get somewhere.

Are you worn and heavy laden,
   Pressed with many a care?
Cast your burden on the Lord, and—
   Get somewhere.

Are you looking for your mission,
   What to do and dare?
Cease your dreaming, start at something—
   Get somewhere.

You will never know His fullness
   Till you boldly dare
To commit your all to Him and—
   Get somewhere.
                    —*A. B. Simpson*

NONE BUT THYSELF

Low at Thy feet, Lord Jesus,
   This is the place for me;
There I have learned sweet lessons,
   Truth that has set me free.

Free from myself, Lord Jesus,
   Free from the ways of men,
Chains of thought that once bound me
   Never shall bind again.

None but Thyself, Lord Jesus,
   Conquered my wayward will;
But for Thy grace, my Saviour,
   I had been wayward still.

WORK

For we are laborers together with God—I Corinthians 3:9

MY TASK

To love some one more dearly every day,
To help a wandering child to find his way,
To ponder o'er a noble thought and pray,
And smile when evening falls—
    This is my task.
To follow truth as blind men seek for light,
To do my best from dawn of day till night,
To keep my heart fit for His holy sight,
And answer when He calls—
    This is my task.

            —Maude Louise Ray

USE EVEN ME

Lord, speak to me, that I may speak
  In living echoes of thy tone;
As thou hast sought, so let me seek
  Thy erring children lost and lone.

O lead me, Lord, that I may lead
  The wandering and the wavering feet;
O feed me, Lord, that I may feed
  Thy hungering ones with manna sweet.

O strengthen me, that while I stand
  Firm on the Rock, and strong in thee,
I may stretch out a loving hand
  To wrestlers with the troubled sea.

O teach me, Lord, that I may teach
   The precious things thou dost impart;
And wing my words, that they may reach
   The hidden depths of many a heart.

O give thine own sweet rest to me,
   That I may speak with soothing power
A word in season, as from thee,
   To weary ones in needful hour.

O fill me with thy fulness, Lord,
   Until my very heart o'erflow
In kindling thought and glowing word,
   Thy love to tell, thy praise to show.

O use me, Lord, use even me,
   Just as thou wilt, and when, and where;
Until thy blessed face I see,
   Thy rest, thy joy, thy glory share.
                    —*Frances Ridley Havergal*

Lord of All Pots and Pans

Lord of all pots and pans and things; since I've no time to be
A saint by doing lovely things or watching late with Thee,
Or dreaming in the dawnlight or storming heaven's gates,
Make me a saint by getting meals, and washing up the plates.

Although I must have Martha's hands, I have a Mary mind;
And when I black the boots and shoes, Thy sandals, Lord, I find.
I think of how they trod the earth, each time I scrub the floor;
Accept this meditation, Lord, I haven't time for more.

Warm all the kitchen with Thy love, and light it with Thy peace;
Forgive me all my worrying, and make my grumbling cease.
Thou Who didst love to give men food, in room or by the sea,
Accept this service that I do—I do it unto Thee.

GIVE ME STRENGTH

Each day I pray high God to give me strength anew
To do the task I do not wish to do;
To love and own the truth and scorn the lie,
To yield obedience, not asking why;
To cheer for those who pass me in the race,
To look a cold world in the face;
To bear my burdens daily, unafraid,
To lend a hand to those that need my aid;
To measure what I am by what I give.
God, give me strength that I may rightly live.

IN A SMALL PLACE

Fret not because thy place is small,
    Thy service need not be,
For thou canst make it all there is
    Of joy and ministry.

The dewdrop, as the boundless sea,
    In God's great plan has part;
And this is all He asks of thee;
    Be faithful *where thou art*.

In thee His mighty hand can show
    The wonders of His grace,
And He can make the humblest room
    A high and holy place.

Thy life can know the blessedness
    Of resting in His will;
His fulness flows unceasingly
    Thy cup of need to fill.

His strength upon thy weakness waits,
    His power for thy task.
What more, O child of all His care,
    Could any great one ask?
        —*Annie Johnson Flint*

In Any Office

My potter's busy wheel is where
I see a desk and office chair,
And well I know the Lord is there.

And all my work is for a King
Who gives His potter songs to sing,
Contented songs, through everything.

And nothing is too small to tell
To Him with whom His potters dwell,
My Counsellor, Emmanuel.

Master, Thy choice is good to me,
It is a happy thing to be,
Here in my office—here with Thee.
    —*Amy Carmichael*

Your Place

Is your place a small place?
    Tend it with care!—
        He set you there.

Is your place a large place?
    Guard it with care!—
        He set you there.

Whate'er your place, it is
    Not yours alone, but His
        Who set you there.
        —*John Oxenham*

Workers with Him

Little is much when God is in it;
Man's busiest day's not worth God's minute;
Much is little everywhere,

If God the labor does not share;
So work with God and nothing's lost;
Who works with Him does best and most:
Work on! Work on!

—*A. A. Rees*

It Is Not the Deed

It is not the deed that we do,
    Tho' the deed be never so fair,
But the love that the dear Lord looketh for,
    Hidden with loving care
    In heart of the deed so fair.

Yes, love is the priceless thing,
    The treasure, our treasure must hold,
Or ever the Master receives the gift,
    Or tells the weight of the gold,
    By the love which cannot be told.

The World's Bible

Christ has no hands but our hands
    To do His work today,
He has no feet but our feet
    To lead men in His way,
He has no tongue but our tongues
    To tell men how He died,
He has no help but our help
    To bring them to His side.

We are the only Bible
    The careless world will read,
We are the sinner's gospel,
    We are the scoffer's creed,
We are the Lord's last message,
    Given in deed and word.

What if the type is crooked?
  What if the print is blurred?

What if our hands are busy
  With other work than His?
What if our feet are walking
  Where sin's allurement is?
What if our tongues are speaking
  Of things His lips would spurn?
How can we hope to help Him
  And hasten His return?
    —*Annie Johnson Flint*

HERE IN MY WORKSHOP

Here in my workshop, where I toil
  Till head and hands are well-nigh spent;
Out on the road where the dust and soil
  Fall thick on garments worn and rent;
Or in the kitchen where I bake
  The bread the little children eat,
He comes: his hand of strength I take,
  And every lonely task grows sweet.

A NURSE'S PRAYER

Because the day that stretches out for me
Is full of busy hours, I come to Thee
To ask Thee, Lord, that Thou wilt see me through
The many things that I may have to do.
Help me to make my beds the smoothest way.
Help me to make more tempting every tray.
Help me to sense when pain must have relief.
Help me to deal with those borne down by grief.
Help me to take to every patient's room
The Light of Life to brighten up the gloom.

Help me to bring to every soul in fear
The sure and steadfast thought that Thou art near.

And if today, or, if tonight, maybe,
Some patient in my care set out to sea
To face the great adventure we call death,
Sustain them, Father, in their parting breath.
Help me to live throughout this live-long day
As one who loves Thee well, dear Lord, I pray;
And when the day is done, and evening stars
Shine through the dark above the sunset bars,
When weary quite, I turn to seek my rest,
Lord, may I truly know I've done my best.
—*Ruth Winant Wheeler*

WORSHIP

*O come, let us worship and bow down: let us kneel
before the Lord our maker*   —*Psalm 95:6*

ONE THING HAVE I DESIRED

One thing have I desired, my God, of Thee,
That will I seek, Thine house be home to me.

I would not breathe an alien, other air,
I would be with Thee, O Thou fairest Fair.

For I would see the beauty of my Lord,
And hear Him speak, who is my heart's Adored.

O Love of loves, and can such wonder dwell
In Thy great Name of names, Immanuel?

Thou with Thy child, Thy child at home with Thee,
O Love of loves, I love, I worship Thee.
—*Amy Carmichael*

It Is Good To Sing Thy Praises

It is good to sing Thy praises and to thank Thee, O Most High,
Showing forth Thy loving kindness when the morning lights the sky.

Thou hast filled my heart with gladness through the works Thy
hands have wrought;
Thou hast made my life victorious, great Thy works and deep Thy
thought.

It is good when night is falling of Thy faithfulness to tell,
While with sweet, melodious praises songs of adoration swell.

In His goodness to the righteous God His righteousness displays;
God my rock, my strength and refuge, just and true are all His
ways.

—Psalm 92

Morning Prayer

Now that the daylight fills the sky,
We lift our hearts to God on high,
That he, in all we do or say,
Would keep us free from harm to-day:

Would guard our hearts and tongues from strife;
From anger's din would hide our life:
From all ill sights would turn our eyes,
Would close our ears from vanities. . . .

So we when this new day is gone,
And night in turn is drawing on,
With conscience by the world unstained
Shall praise his name for victory gained.

All laud to God the Father be;
All praise, eternal Son, to thee;
All glory, as is ever meet,
To God the holy Paraclete.

Evening Prayer

Before the ending of the day,
Creator of the world, we pray
That with thy wonted favour thou
Wouldst be our Guard and Keeper now.

From all ill dreams defend our eyes,
From mighty fears and fantasies;
Tread under foot our ghostly foe,
That no pollution we may know.

O Father, this we ask be done,
Through Jesus Christ, thine only Son;
Who, with the Holy Ghost and thee,
Doth live and reign eternally.

From The Meeting

And so I find it well to come
For deeper rest to this still room,
For here the habit of the soul
Feels less the outer world's control;
For strength of mutual purpose pleads
More earnestly our common needs;
And from the silence multiplied
By these still forms on either side,
The world that time and sense have known
Falls off and leaves us God alone.

—John Greenleaf Whittier

No East or West

In Christ there is no East or West,
    In Him no South or North,
But one great Fellowship of Love
    Throughout the whole wide earth.

In Him shall true hearts everywhere
    Their high communion find.
His service is the golden cord
    Close-binding all mankind.

Join hands then, Brothers of the Faith,
    Whate'er your race may be!—
Who serves my Father as a son
    Is surely kin to me.

In Christ now meet both East and West,
    In Him meet South and North,
All Christly souls are one in Him,
    Throughout the whole wide earth.
                —*John Oxenham*

YOUTH

*And the streets of the city shall be full of boys and
girls playing in the streets thereof—Zechariah 8:5*

FOR OUR CHILDREN

Father, hear us, we are praying,
Hear the words our hearts are saying,
We are praying for our children.

Keep them from the powers of evil,
From the secret, hidden peril,
From the whirlpool that would suck them,
From the treacherous quicksand, pluck them.

From the worldling's hollow gladness,
From the sting of faithless sadness,
Holy Father, save our children.

Through life's troubled waters steer them,
Through life's bitter battle cheer them,

Father, Father, be Thou near them.
Read the language of our longing,
Read the wordless pleadings thronging,
Holy Father, for our children.

And wherever they may bide,
Lead them Home at eventide.
                    —Amy Carmichael

From IN THE BLEAK MID-WINTER

What can I give Him,
  Poor as I am?
If I were a shepherd
  I would bring a lamb,
If I were a Wise Man
  I would do my part,—
Yet what I can I give Him,
  Give my heart.
              —Christina Rossetti

A CHILD'S PRAYER

Lamb of God, I look to thee;
Thou shalt my Example be;
Thou art gentle, meek and mild,
Thou wast once a little child.

Fain I would be as thou art;
Give me thy obedient heart.
Thou art pitiful and kind;
Let me have thy loving mind . . .

Thou didst live to God alone,
Thou didst never seek thine own;
Thou thyself didst never please.
God was all thy happiness.

Loving Jesus, gentle Lamb,
In thy gracious hands I am,
Make me, Saviour, what thou art,
Live thyself within my heart.
                    —*Charles Wesley*

CONSECRATION

Just as I am, Thine own to be,
Friend of the young, who lovest me,
To consecrate myself to Thee,
O Jesus Christ, I come.

In the glad morning of my day,
My life I give, my vows to pay,
With no reserve and no delay,
With all my heart I come.

I would live ever in the light,
I would work ever for the right,
I would serve Thee with all my might;
Therefore, to Thee, I come.

Just as I am, young, strong, and free,
To be the best that I can be
For truth, and righteousness and Thee,
Lord of my life, I come.
                    —*Marianne Hearn*

A CHILD'S PRAYER

Little Jesus, wast Thou shy
Once, and just as small as I?
And what did it feel like to be
Out of Heaven, and just like me?
Didst Thou sometimes think of *there,*
And ask where all the angels were?
I should think that I would cry

For my house all made of sky;
I would look about the air,
And wonder where my angels were;
And at waking 'twould distress me—
Not an angel there to dress me!

Hadst Thou ever any toys,
Like us little girls and boys?
And didst Thou play in Heaven with all
The Angels, that were not too tall,
With stars for marbles? Did the things
Play *Can you see me?* through their wings?

Didst Thou kneel at night to pray,
And didst Thou join Thy hands, this way?
And did they tire sometimes, being young,
And make the prayer seem very long?
And dost Thou like it best, that we
Should join our hands and pray to Thee?
I used to think, before I knew,
The prayer not said unless we do.
And did Thy Mother at the night
Kiss Thee and fold the clothes in right?
And didst Thou feel quite good in bed,
Kissed, and sweet, and Thy prayers said?

Thou canst not have forgotten all
That it feels like to be small:
And Thou know'st I cannot pray
To Thee in my father's way—
When Thou wast so little, say,
Could'st Thou talk Thy Father's way?—
So, a little child, come down
And hear a child's tongue like Thy own;
Take me by the hand and walk,
And listen to my baby-talk.
To Thy Father show my prayer
(He will look, Thou art so fair),

And say: "O Father, I, Thy son,
Bring the prayer of a little one."

And He will smile, that children's tongue
Has not changed since Thou wast young!
                    —*Francis Thompson*

PRAYER AT A NURSERY WINDOW

So brief a time I have them, Lord,
To steady them with Thy bright word;
A narrow span of childish days
To set their feet in Thy great ways—
A few swift nights to know them warm,
Close-gathered now from any harm,
Looming in shadowy years ahead . . .
How can I help but be afraid?

The little wisdom I have won
Is not enough to guard my son.
The grace I grope for, deed by deed,
Cannot assuage my daughter's need;
Nor wit, nor courage hold at bay
The moment, that imperiled day,
For which no foresight may prepare—
Nor even love, not even prayer.

Be to them, God, all I would be
In that far time I shall not see;
And guide me now, their friend, their mother,
To hear their prayers, to smooth the cover,
And leave their windows wide upthrust
Beneath that Heaven of my trust,
Whose pity marked a sparrow's fall
And bends in mercy over all.
                    —*Frances Stoakley Lankford*

THE TEACHER

Lord, who am I to teach the way
    To little children day by day,
So prone myself to go astray?

I teach them knowledge, but I know
    How faint they flicker and how low
The candles of my knowledge glow.

I teach them power to will and do,
    But only now to learn anew
My own great weakness thru and thru

I teach them love for all mankind
    And all God's creatures, but I find
My love comes lagging far behind.

Lord, if their guide I still must be,
    Oh, let the little children see
The teacher leaning hard on Thee.
                    —*Leslie Pinckney Hill*

THE BRIDGE BUILDER

An old man traveling a lone highway,
Came at the evening cold and gray,
To a chasm vast and deep and wide,
Through which was flowing a sullen tide
The old man crossed in the twilight dim,
The sullen stream held no fears for him
But he turned when safe on the other side
And builded a bridge to span the tide.

"Old man," cried a fellow pilgrim near,
"You're wasting your time in building here.
Your journey will end with the closing day;
You never again will pass this way.
You have crossed the chasm deep and wide,
Why build you this bridge at even-tide?"

The builder lifted his old gray head:
"Good friend, in the path I have come," he said,
"There followeth after me today
A youth whose feet must pass this way.
This stream which has been as naught to me,
To that fair-haired youth may pitfall be.
He, too, must cross in the twilight dim—
Good friend, I am building this bridge for him."
                            —*Will Allen Dromgoole*

TELL ME, MOTHER

Tell me, Mother, what is fire?
And how do bluebirds fly?
Tell me which you think is higher,
Heaven or the sky?

Are there really stars in snow?
Do willows often weep?
Tell me, Mother, where I go
When I go to sleep?

In awe and wonder I have stood
Before his lifted eyes,
And prayed that I may make him good
As well as wise!
                            —*Sybil Leonard Armes*

Index of Authors

Index of First Lines

Index of Titles